The
FIVEFOLD
MINISTRY
Gifts
Apostle, Prophet, Evangelist, Pastor, Teacher

Dirk Waren

The FIVEFOLD MINISTRY Gifts: Apostle, Prophet, Evangelist, Pastor, Teacher

ISBN: 979-8-218-02673-8
PUBLISHED BY SOARING EAGLE PRESS
Youngstown

Printed in the United States of America

So Christ himself gave the apostles, the prophets, the evangelists, the pastors and teachers, to equip his people for works of service, so that the body of Christ may be built up.

- Ephesians 4:11-12

CONTENTS

Introduction

The Purpose of this Book

This isn't just a handbook for Christian ministers and aspiring ministers but also a handbook for believers in general so they can understand the various types of ministers and what each of the five ministry gifts has to offer.

Not every minister is a pastor who oversees a local assembly and performs weddings or funerals. We have to get away from this one-dimensional idea because it's simply not biblical.

Just as important, this book reveals the prime directive of Christian ministers — their goal: To encourage and spiritually feed people through the ministry of the word, assist in their spiritual development, and prepare them for the specific works of service to which God calls them in the body of Christ.

We'll also look at what ministers are *not* supposed to do, such as lord it over people and therefore abuse them spiritually, mentally or physically. In other words, this is a *balanced* study that stresses the good of ministers and ministry, but also honestly looks at the bad and foolish.

When you understand these things it'll set you free from religious myths about ministers and ministry, not to mention protect ministers from burn-out and people in general from potential manipulation or mistreatment. As the Lord said, "The truth will make you free."

PART I

The Fivefold Ministry Gifts

This first section of the book focuses on the five different ministerial gifts that God has provided for the worldwide Church. It will help you to distinguish these anointings as well as receive from them and enhance your spiritual growth.

1

What are the Fivefold Ministry Gifts?

When people hear the term 'minister' they naturally think of a pastor, a minister who oversees a local assembly, big or small, and usually performs weddings and funerals. Yet pastoring is only one of the five ministerial gifts in the body of Christ. This is observed in this passage:

> **So Christ himself gave the <u>apostles</u>, the <u>prophets</u>, the <u>evangelists</u>, the <u>pastors</u> and <u>teachers</u>, [12] to equip his people for works of service, so that the body of Christ may be built up [13] until we all reach unity in the faith and in the knowledge of the Son of God and become mature, attaining to the whole measure of the fullness of Christ.**
>
> **Ephesians 4:11-13**

Jesus Christ is the Head of the global Church (Ephesians 1:22 & Colossians 1:18) and thus it is the Lord who distributes these five ministry gifts to whom he chooses. These are anointings, aka spiritual talents, graciously given to those called to these positions in the body of Christ. A friend of mine is currently going to Bible school and asked a great local pastor how he was able to consistently put together insightful teachings that feed & inspire so many believers. The minister simply replied, "It's a gift."

While these five ministry gifts are distinguished, they have the same general purpose:

- To equip or prepare people for works of service (i.e. ministry).
- To build up the body of Christ and the members thereof (not tear them down, although there's certainly a place for proper correction).
- To facilitate a spirit of unity in the faith and knowledge of the Lord (as opposed to a spirit of rigid sectarianism).
- To assist believers in growing spiritually (not stagnating and becoming lifeless religionists).
- To help believers attain to the whole measure of the fullness of Christ (as opposed to a quarter measure or half measure).

Needless to say, every servant-leader in the worldwide Church — whether apostle, prophet, evangelist, pastor or teacher — needs to make sure they're fulfilling these purposes and not doing the opposite.

To accomplish this mission, all fivefold ministers naturally need to:

1. **Know and walk with the LORD** (John 17:3 & Ephesians 1:17).
2. **Know the Word of God** (John 8:31-32), not to mention be able to teach or preach it.

Teaching refers to careful instruction of scriptural truth whereas **preaching** is proclamation of God's Word in an exhortative sense, which means to encourage or motivate people (Acts 15:35 & 1 Timothy 5:17). Simply put, teaching **spiritually feeds** the listener or reader while preaching **inspires them to action**, whether that is to practice what's being taught (if it's a practical truth) or to change one's mindset (if it's a revelational truth).

It goes without saying that **1.** knowing God and **2.** knowing God's Word are both mandatory for servant-leaders in the body of Christ for obvious reasons (Luke 13:24-27, Matthew 7:15-23 & 1 Corinthians 4:6).

Helping members of the Church reach a place of unity in faith and knowledge would obviously include teaching & preaching accurate doctrine so that believers are not misled by false teachings.

It should be stressed that the minister's Prime Directive is to prepare believers so that *they themselves* can serve effectively in the body of Christ in their unique place in the world. This is the result of feeding them the Word of God (Matthew 4:4), exhorting them and setting an example for them.

With this understanding, fivefold ministers should not be viewed as hired hands who perform tasks *in place of* the believer. Rather, they are servant-leaders who train & inspire believers to perform those tasks themselves. For instance, why call a minister to go to the hospital and pray with a relative or friend when you can just do it yourself, assuming you're equipped to do so?

For instance, Christ's ministry consisted of teaching, preaching and healing (Matthew 4:23 & 9:35), but once people believed the gospel he trained them and sent them out to minister to others themselves (Matthew 10:1, Mark 6:7-13 & Luke 10).

You probably noticed that I referred to fivefold ministers as *servant*-leaders. The reason for this is…

Fivefold Ministers are to be *Servant*-Leaders, Not Domineering Authoritarians

Believers with one or more of the fivefold ministry gifts are called to be servant-leaders in the body of Christ. They're leaders, no doubt, but their style of leadership is servant-oriented rather than authoritarian. The Lord made this clear:

> **Jesus called them** [the disciples] **together and said, "You know that the rulers of the Gentiles lord it over them, and their high officials exercise authority over them. [26]<u>Not so with you</u>. Instead, whoever wants to become great among you must be your <u>servant</u>, [27]and whoever wants to be first must be your <u>slave</u> — [28] just as the Son of Man did not come to be served, <u>but to serve</u>, and to give his life as a ransom for many."**
>
> **Matthew 20:25-28**

> **The greatest among you will be your <u>servant</u>. [12]For those who exalt themselves will be humbled, and those who humble themselves will be exalted.** **Matthew 23:11-12**

> **They came to Capernaum. When he was in the house, he asked them, "What were you arguing about on the road?" [34]But they kept quiet because on the way <u>they had argued about who was the greatest</u>.**

³⁵Sitting down, Jesus called the Twelve and said, <u>"Anyone who wants to be first must be the very last, and the servant of all</u>."

Mark 9:33-35

The word 'minister' literally means "servant" and so fivefold ministers are to minister with a servant's heart. This doesn't mean, of course, that ministers should be overly nice milksops as there's a time and place for *tough* love, like when Paul openly challenged Peter's legalism (Galatians 2:11-14) or when Christ amazingly cleansed the Temple of fools (Mark 11:15-18) or when Peter rebuked a sorcerer in Samaria (Acts 8:9-24).

Fivefold Ministers are to Build Believers Up, <u>Not</u> Tear Down

We saw above that fivefold ministers are "to prepare God's people for works of service, so that the body of Christ may be **built up**" (Ephesians 4:11-13). In other words, genuine ministers — and believers in general — are to overflow with life, not death. Why? Because we're children of God and the LORD is the Fountain of Life (Psalm 36:9). This explains Christ's mission: **to give people life and life to the full**, not death (John 10:10).

This is not to say that there's no place for condemning sin and inspiring repentance when ministering. Capable ministers who are anointed of the Spirit will bring about a spirit of repentance via **the ministry of the Word** (Acts 6:1-4), but will also remove the weight of guilt, impart God's peace and spur people forward. In short, even though they condemn sin and encourage repentance, their ministry is inspiring and encouraging. This is the minister's job.

A good example of this can be observed in the Scriptures. After Christ's resurrection, he appeared to a couple of the disciples who were naturally disheartened in the wake of his undue execution. The Messiah suddenly joined them as they were traveling and they talked for a while, but they failed to recognize him. After Jesus left, the two reflected on this meeting: "Were not **our hearts burning within us** while he talked with us on the road and opened the Scriptures to us?" (Luke 24:32).

This is the kind of effect true ministers will have on people. You know you're at a fit fellowship when you depart with your heart burning with encouragement and you have fresh revelation from God's Word you never saw before.

If, on the other hand, you leave an assembly feeling beat up, weighed down and condemned, it's not good. It shows that the minister executing the service has become infected by a form of legalism and is spiritually toxic. Such a spirit of condo is at odds with the true ministerial spirit, which Paul summed up when he noted the authority ministers have for **building believers up and not tearing them down** (2 Corinthians 10:8 & 13:10).

We'll look at the spirit of condemnation & authoritarianism further in chapter **13**.

So what distinguishes these five ministerial gifts — apostle, prophet, evangelist, pastor and teacher? Let's now briefly look at each one in general terms (as a small book could easily be written on each)…

2

The Gift of APOSTLE

The word 'apostle' is *apostolos (ah-POS-tol-os)* in the original Greek, which means "one sent on a mission with a message." All disciples of Christ have this mission, of course, as the Lord instructed the disciples: "Therefore go and make disciples of all nations, baptizing them in the name of the Father and of the Son and of the Holy Spirit, and teaching them to obey everything I have commanded you" (Matthew 28:19-20). However, apostles like Paul and John had an anointing to go out and *start* assemblies, as well as *oversee* them. In order to start fellowships, an apostle obviously has to have the gift of pastoring.

A good modern example of an apostle is this powerful minister in my area who started a very successful fellowship, which then sprouted satellite fellowships all over the region. He eventually stopped pastoring the main assembly and took the position of "bishop," overseeing all of these assemblies (we'll look at this particular term in chapter 7). This certainly sounds like operating in the gift of an apostle, doesn't it?

Paul also said that a true apostle is marked by "signs, wonders and miracles" (2 Corinthians 12:12). But this might be hard to come by in these days of gross unbelief.[1] Thankfully, I've seen modern apostles minister in this capacity; they're out there.

If there are "true apostles" there are also "false apostles" (2 Corinthians 11:13-14). I once met a joyless, stern believer who insisted on being addressed as "Apostle Harrad" at all times even though he wasn't remotely an apostle in any biblical sense.

How much of the above has to be relevant for a minister to be considered a true apostle? They'd have to:

1. Have a drive for reaching people with the Word of God and starting fellowships,
2. Oversee several assemblies (at least more than one),
3. Have an anointing with the laying on of hands. If you're not familiar with the laying on of hands, it's the 4th doctrine of Christianity (Hebrews 6:1-2).[2]

---

[1] See the **Appendix** for one key reason *why* there's so much unbelief in this particular area.

[2] For details get my book *The SIX BASIC DOCTRINES of Christianity* or see the corresponding article at the Fountain of Life (FOL) site and scroll down to the section *4. The Laying on of Hands.*

3

The Gift of PROPHET

The word 'prophet' in the Greek is *prophétés (prah-FAY-tus)* which means "an interpreter or forth-teller of the divine will." Please don't confuse this wonderful gift with that of an occultist fortune teller.

The prophetic word is encouraging and is able to **touch believers in that specific area where they need ministered**. For example, Acts 15:32 says, "Judas and Silas, who themselves were prophets, said much to encourage and strengthen the believers." This is the purpose of the prophetic gift in the Church and reveals why it is so necessary — **it encourages and strengthens believers**.

The original Greek word for 'encourage' in this passage means "**to cause to move forward**." In other words, a prophetic word will **inspire believers** and **provoke them to go forward and fulfill God's call on their lives**. This shows that prophets are more preachers than teachers. They see things in the spirit realm and proclaim God's will that's applicable to the situation or person, but they don't go into scriptural details on doctrine, like a teacher would.

Have you ever been in the spiritual doldrums where you're not necessarily walking in sin, but you just seem to lack that spiritual drive and passion for the Lord and your calling? The gift of prophecy has the ability to wake believers from such lethargy and spark them onward!

It's an awesome gift and a needed gift. As such, the office of the prophet should be valued and esteemed in the Church. Unfortunately, too many assemblies and sects are ignorant of it or the gift lies dormant for various reasons, which we'll address in chapter 7.

I'd like to offer a recent example of how a Spirit-anointed prophetic word can encourage the believer. I was discouraged about what was happening in the political realm after reading the Eeyore-like commentaries of a couple of ministers who, while certainly respectable and gifted as teachers, lacked prophetic insight. Listening to them produced the vibe of "Woe are we as a nation; our sins have brought doom despite the millions upon millions of sincere, fruit-bearing saints in Christ and their many prayers."

I then exposed myself to four mighty men & women of God who flowed in the prophetic word. Unlike the other two downbeat ministers, these prophets inspired and encouraged me. This isn't to say, of course, that there isn't a time & place for a sobering prophetic correction from the Lord, like Christ did with the Laodicean assembly (Revelation 3:17).

While the word of prophecy is essential in the Church this does not condone the abuse of this gift where believers are made to feel like they're captive to a prophetic word that may be off or even wholly wrong. Nor does it condone the authoritarian behavior of prophets who think their prophecies are the inerrant Word of God which must be blindly embraced and followed to the letter.

The cause of this kind of abusive error is believers confusing the New Testament prophet with the Old Testament prophet. These two types of biblical prophets are quite different. The primary purpose of the Old Testament prophet was to lead and guide Israel through the proclamation of the Word of the LORD and, in fact, a lot of their words became Holy Scripture and are included in what we know today as the Old Testament.

Jesus Christ *was the final individual to function in the anointing of an Old Testament prophet* (Hebrews 1:1-2). As a matter of fact, he was *The* Prophet that the Hebrews were expecting for almost 1500 years (Deuteronomy 18:15, John 6:14 & 7:40).

The New Testament prophet is different from the Old Testament prophet. The gift of prophecy was not given to the body of Christ for the purpose of leading and guiding God's people, as was the case in the Old Covenant, because believers are spiritually regenerated and have the Holy Ghost within them for this very purpose.

As Jesus said, "But when he, the Spirit of truth, comes, he will guide you into all truth. He will not speak on his own; he will speak only what he hears, and he will tell you what is yet to come" (John16:13). Since it is the Holy Spirit's job to guide believers in the New Testament era, we don't need the gift of prophecy for this function.

So when a prophet prophesies over you and says you're to do this or that and go here or there, don't receive it unless the Spirit has *already* been leading you in this direction. In other words, prophecies in the New Testament are to *confirm* what the Holy

Spirit has *already* been leading you to do. You could say it's an external source to confirm or compliment the believer's internal source of direction from God.

This explains why Paul instructed believers to *test* prophecies and "hold on to the good," which means to eat the meat and spit out the bones (1 Thessalonians 5:19-21). Nowhere are we instructed to *blindly* accept a prophecy spoken over us.

For important details on these issues see chapter **16**.

4

The Gift of EVANGELIST

'Evangelist' in the Greek is *euaggelistés (yoo-ang-ghel-is-TAYS)*, which means "a bringer of good news." Like prophets, they're preachers and not teachers. They proclaim by unction the truths of the gospel and the Word of God in general, but they're not effective at detail-oriented teaching.

Many hardcore missionaries would be examples of fivefold evangelists (by 'hardcore' I mean those who function as missionaries in a vocational sense as opposed to those who flirt with missionary work for relatively short periods of time, usually because their sect sends them out for mandatory field work). While *euaggelistés* only appears three times in the Greek scriptures, the verb form, *euaggelizó (yoo-ang-ghel-ID-zoh)*, appears 54 times.

Evangelists can certainly minister to *believers* at revivals and what have you, but their drive & focus is reaching the lost with the life-changing Good News of the message of Christ (2 Corinthians 5:17-21).

I knew a pastor who simultaneously had the gift of an evangelist, which was also the case with Timothy (2 Timothy 4:5). This particular pastor wasn't good at teaching, although he could preach and — as a pastor — he was gifted at overseeing an assembly. I saw him at an evangelical service and he was exceptional at preaching the gospel and inspiring people to turn to the Lord in repentance and faith (Acts 20:21). In fact, my aged father got saved at one of his evangelistic services. This shows that ministers can have more than one of the fivefold gifts, although only Jesus Christ functioned in all five of them.

Like apostles and prophets, evangelists in the New Testament were known to flow in the gifts of the Spirit, such as Philip (Acts 8:4-7, 8:26-40 & 21:8).

5

The Gift of PASTOR

The word 'pastor' comes from the Greek *poimén (poy-MAYN)* meaning "shepherd," whether literally in reference to a shepherd of sheep (Luke 2:8) or figuratively in the sense of someone overseeing a 'flock' of people. In the latter sense, Christ is the "Good Shepherd" of the Church (John 10:11,14,27) while fivefold ministers with the gift of pastoring are under-shepherds, as observed in this passage:

> **To the elders among you, I appeal as a fellow elder and a witness of Christ's sufferings who also will share in the glory to be revealed: [2] Be shepherds of God's flock that is under your care, watching over them** — not because you must, **but because you are willing, as God wants you to be; not pursuing dishonest gain, but eager to serve; [3] not lording it over those entrusted to you, but being examples to the flock. [4] And when the Chief Shepherd appears, you will receive the crown of glory that will never fade away.**
>
> **1 Peter 5:1-4**

Peter was an elder and an apostle and he is addressing elders here, but specifically pastors, as shown in verse 2 (the word 'shepherds' in the Greek is the verb form of *poimén*). In verse 4 he notes that Christ is the *Chief* Shepherd, which shows that pastors are *under-shepherds*, accountable to the Lord.

Verses 2-3 convey Peter's six instructions to pastors. They are to:

1. **"Shepherd God's flock** that is under your care," which is phrased in the KJV as **"Feed the flock of God"** (1 Peter 5:2). This corresponds to what Christ instructed Peter (John 21:15-17). Making sure the believers under their care are spiritually fed is the number one duty of pastors, which includes exposing them to the ministry of other fivefold ministers now & then so that they'll be "fully equipped for every good work" (Ephesians 4:12). Feeding believers the word of God is called "the ministry of the word" (Acts 6:1-4). Notice, by the way, that those believers under the pastor's care are called **"God's** flock." In other words, believers in the worldwide Church are *God's* sheep, not the pastor's sheep. The pastor merely shepherds certain believers for the period of time they are under that pastor's care, which isn't determined by the pastor, but by the believer, as led of the Holy Spirit.

2. **"Watch over"** those believers who are under your care, that is, **oversee them**. This means to supervise or manage the believers under their care in a protective and directive sense, but it *doesn't* mean to tyrannically dominate them in an authoritarian sense (more on this momentarily).

3. **Don't pursue dishonest gain**, which means don't be greedy. Christian ministers in general cannot simultaneously be lovers of money, aka lucre-worshipers (Matthew 6:24, 1 Timothy 3:3 & Titus 1:7). Why? Because people obsessed with money and materialism will naturally

take advantage of their position to manipulate others in order to acquire the object of their love, lucre. Even deacons cannot be greedy, which refers to those in helps ministry (1 Timothy 3:8).[3]

4. **Be eager to serve rather than begrudgingly serve.** If a fivefold minister cannot pastor people with gratefulness and enthusiasm he should do something else in God's service.

5. **Don't "lord it over" those entrusted to you**, which means don't be a pompous authoritarian. Pastors who lord it over those in their assemblies try to control or subjugate them in the sense of being the ultimate authority. The problem with this is that they aren't the supreme authority, God is. If you're a pastor, please don't be like this; serve with a loving, humble servant's heart. Anyone functioning in the office of pastor who cannot do this, needs to find another way to serve in the kingdom.

6. **Be examples to "the flock" in all you say and do.** This shows that ministry isn't just about "the ministry of the Word of God" (Acts 6:1-4), but also actually walking with the Lord and walking in newness of life. In short, it's not just talking the talk, it's walking the walk. Talk is cheap.

When the **elders** of the assembly of Ephesus met Paul in Miletus, he instructed them to "Keep watch over yourselves and all the flock of which the Holy Spirit has made you **overseers**. Be **shepherds** [pastors] of the church of God, which he bought with his own blood" (Acts 20:28). This shows that elders (*presbuteros*), overseers (*episkopos*) and pastors (*poimén*) are synonymous in the New Testament.

---

[3] For more on the position of deacon see chapter **17**.

In other words, they refer to the same office, although "elder" could refer to another fivefold minister; for instance, the apostle John was nicknamed "the elder" when he was mature in years (2 John 1:1 & 3 John 1:1). (A nickname is a nickname, not a title; for instance, one pastor I knew was called Butch, even though his name was Bob). Also, an overseer could refer to an apostle since apostles start out as pastors and eventually oversee several assemblies. Even prophets, evangelists and teachers are overseers of the inner circle of their ministries.

Should Ministers Be Paid for Their Services?

Ideally, those effective elders in the Church who preach and teach should be well paid (1 Corinthians 9:14). They are "worthy of double honor" the Bible says (1 Timothy 5:17). The Greek for 'honor' in this verse is a financial term.

However, fivefold ministers might have to take up secular work to pay the bills, which is what Paul occasionally did by making tents (Acts 18:3-5). Paul didn't take collections from the believers in Corinth as a voluntary sacrifice on their behalf (1 Corinthians 9:12,18). He was only able to do this without resorting to secular work because he was receiving finances from other assemblies under his apostleship (2 Corinthians 11:8).

What about Old Testament ministers, did they receive payment for their services? Keep in mind that the accounts of the Hebrews chronicled in the Old Testament serve as lessons to us, the worldwide Church (Romans 15:4 & 1 Corinthians 10:11). Here are three examples of ministers being respected by people offering financial support in one form or another:

1. Young Saul (before he became king) and his servant insisted on honorably paying Samuel for his services (1 Samuel 9:6-8).
2. The first king of the Northern Kingdom of Israel, Jeroboam, made sure his wife paid the prophet Ahijah with gifts for his services (1 Kings 14:1-3).
3. The mighty prophet Elisha was rewarded for his services (2 Kings 4:42 & 5:15).

Pastors Who *Teach* and Pastors Who *Preach*

As noted in chapter **1**, all fivefold ministers must know the Word of God and be able to teach or preach so that the body of Christ is fed & exhorted spiritually at gatherings. Pastors also require the gift to *oversee* an assembly of believers (apostles too, obviously). I've been to some assemblies where the pastors are outstanding at teaching God's Word, which means carefully explaining topics in an insightful, inspiring manner. However, I've been to other fellowships where the pastors aren't good at teaching, although they can preach and, like all genuine pastors, are good at overseeing a group of believers.

Obviously pastors who are also exceptional at teaching God's Word have the fivefold gift of a teacher. Pastors who aren't gifted at teaching are effective at preaching and are going to have to enlist the services of fivefold teachers at their assemblies in order to effectively feed God's sheep in their midst. Speaking of teachers…

<u>6</u>

The Gift of TEACHER

'Teacher' in the Greek is *didaskalos (di-DAS-kal-os)*, which simply means "instructor." Fivefold teachers have the anointing to carefully explain the Holy Scriptures in an understandable, enlightening way. They make the Scriptures come alive for their hearers/readers and help them to see things in God's Word they've never seen before.

They give structure to knowledge and their potent insights often result in folks thinking, "I've never heard this, but it makes total sense. Where did the minister get this?!" This is the reaction people had to Christ when he taught (Mark 6:2). It is teaching from the Scriptures that *feeds* people spiritually (Matthew 4:4).

Fivefold teachers differ from pastors (and apostles) in that they don't have the gift of oversight. I'm a fivefold teacher. I have the gift to teach believers, but not oversee them. To be an effective pastor you have to *want* to watch over people. I have no such desire. I operate in the ministry of the word (Acts 6:1-4) and pray for my hearers/readers and then it's in the Spirit's hands, as well as the hands of their local pastor.

I should point out that there is such a thing as a body teacher in the Church (Romans 12:6-8). Such believers have a gift to teach in the body of Christ, but they lack the anointing of a fivefold teacher. These may be fivefold teachers in seedling form, although not necessarily. As they grow spiritually the LORD will eventually lead them into the fivefold ministry. That's what happened with me.

One pastor I know taught that fivefold teachers usually focus on one topic and teach it wherever they minister. This, of course, enables them to become experts at teaching that particular subject. This is not wholly accurate, however. Teachers are typically well-studied on myriad topics — hundreds actually — and can effectively teach them all.

Yet it is true that a teacher may be led by the Spirit to focus on one particular topic and serve people accordingly. For instance, I know a fulltime minister who has about 75 gigs a year and he sticks to one basic topic with four sermons within that context, which means he'd have to be scheduled at the same assembly four times before even considering coming up with something different. Needless to say, if a minister sticks to one topic and four sermons within that topic, they'll get good at it.

7

The Fivefold Ministry Office

So now you understand the five biblically-based servant-leadership positions in the Church — **apostle**, **prophet**, **evangelist**, **pastor** and **teacher**.

In many camps, unfortunately, only the offices of the pastor, teacher and evangelist are active. The other two are pretty much dormant. They might have apostles in some partial form, albeit under a different name and usually minus signs and wonders (2 Corinthians 12:12). Meanwhile they omit the office of prophet altogether.

Some of these sects justify this due to their adherence to the erroneous doctrine of cessationism, the belief that the gifts of the Spirit (1 Corinthians 12:4-11) ceased by the end of the 1st Century when the last of the original apostles passed away. (They curiously include Paul even though he wasn't one of the original apostles). If gifts of the Spirit no longer exist in the Church then obviously an apostle cannot function in signs and wonders and a prophet cannot prophesy, which would make these gifts inoperable and irrelevant.

You can search in vain throughout all the above New Testament passages, but you'll find no statement where the Spirit-led writers of the Scriptures say something like: "However, the positions of the apostle and prophet will only last a little while longer — till the end of this century, in fact — then they will cease, along with the nine gifts of the Spirit."

On the contrary, believers are encouraged to **"eagerly desire"** spiritual gifts, as shown in 1 Corinthians 12:1, 31, 14:1, 39, which would include the gift of personal tongues, otherwise known as glossolalia *(gloss-ah-LAY-lee-ah)*. Paul emphasized eagerly desiring — *pursuing* — the "greater gifts" (1 Corinthians 12:31). What is the greater gift? Simply the specific gift that's needed at the time!

Think about it: The religious doctrine of cessationism encourages believers to do the ***precise opposite*** of what the New Testament Scriptures actually instruct us to do. It encourages believers to *eagerly deny* spiritual gifts when God's Word encourages us to **eagerly desire** them!

That said, while cessationism is a false doctrine, it's not an issue of eternal salvation. If a believer or sect embraces this doctrine it doesn't mean that they're not fellow believers, loved by the Lord. It just means their faith — their belief level based on the false doctrine of cessationism — won't allow them to "eat everything" the gospel of Christ has to offer; in this case, spiritual gifts and the blessings thereof. (Romans 14:1-6).

Those of us with fuller understanding are not to look down on those with the lesser because it would be arrogant. Similarly, the one with the lesser revelation must not condemn the one with the fuller. On the contrary, we are to "accept one another... just as Christ accepted [us], in order to bring praise to God" (Romans

15:7). You could insert any non-essential doctrine or issue into this scenario and it would apply.

The **<u>Appendix</u>** offers further details.

Church of Christ — What Is It?

Since "the Church" has been mentioned several times now I think we should define the Church of Jesus Christ from a biblical standpoint.

The word 'church' in the Greek is *ekklesia (ee-KLEE-see-ah)*, meaning "called out of " or "the called-out ones." It refers to *people* who have been called out of the darkness of this world and consecrated to the LORD by responding to the message of Christ in faith & repentance (Acts 20:21) and the resulting spiritual rebirth (James 1:18). The worldwide Church is synonymous with "the body of Christ" (Colossians 1:18) and is also called "God's household" or "the household of God" (1 Timothy 3:15). **The Church includes every genuine believer who's experienced spiritual regeneration regardless of what sectarian tag they favor** (Titus 3:5).

(Speaking of sectarian tags, please keep this in mind: Putting a label of 'beans' on a can of corn does not make the corn a can of beans. Chew on that).

In its singular form *ekklesia* is used to describe all people in Christ across the planet and not to a specific sect — like, say, the Baptists, Nazarenes or Assemblies of God. When pluralized, *ekklesia* is used in reference to specific assemblies of believers who meet together. In the 1st Century this was often at a person's home (Acts 20:20 & Romans 16:3,5).

It should be noted that *ekklesia*, 'church,' is never used in the Scriptures to describe either a physical facility or a human-organized group — i.e. a sect or denomination — although the people of such an organization may, of course, be the Church ("called-out ones"); and usually are if it's a legitimate ministry organization.

No *specific* assembly or denomination is necessarily the "one true church" because the body of Christ is not a human-organized institution, but rather **a spiritual entity comprised of those who have been reconciled to the LORD by grace through faith** (Ephesians 2:8–9 & 2 Corinthians 5:18-20). Such people — no matter what place they meet at, no matter which camp they're a part of, and no matter what nation they happen to live in — are the true Church.

Any time you hear a minister or believer talk about his or her sect/assembly as the "one true church" it's an indication of the infection of staunch sectarianism, which is a spiritually immature mindset, as witnessed in Jesus' disciples in Luke 9:49-50.

Worse, it's actually a work of the flesh, as shown in Galatians 5:19-21 where "factions" is listed as one of the works of the sinful nature, also translated as "sects." "Factions" or "sects" is a translation of the Greek word *hairesis (HAH-ee-res-is)*, which means "a religious or philosophical sect" and the resulting division or contention in the body of Christ. As such, some translations render the word as "divisions," like the English Standard Version. It's a "self-chose opinion" rooted in sectarian loyalty — i.e. one's favored sect — rather than a viewpoint rooted in the rightly-divided Word of God.

With the understanding of the above, **I** am the Church and **you** are the Church; that is, if you're a genuinely born-anew believer.[4]

What's in a Name?

As suggested in chapter **5**, anyone who functions in one of the five ministry positions — apostle, prophet, evangelist, pastor and teacher — could be called an elder as well and, in some cases, an overseer. The Greek word for 'overseer' *(episkopos)* is also translated as 'bishop' in some English versions of the Bible, such as the KJV. A bishop in the Church is a fivefold minister who oversees a group of subordinate believers.

During my formative years as a young believer, the assembly that I was involved with embraced these five biblical terms for the offices of servant-leaders. I think it's best to stick to biblical terminology since the Holy Scriptures are our basis for doctrinal truth and practice (1 Corinthians 4:6 & 2 Timothy 3:16).

However, if a camp/sect/assembly chooses to use a *different* term for a fivefold minister — whether the minister is called to be an apostle, prophet, evangelist, pastor or teacher — it would not change the fact that the minister functions within the position of one of these five offices. Are you following? In short, it's nothing worth arguing about.

Fivefold Ministers, Great and Small

Fivefold ministers can be great or small and it doesn't change the fact that they are indeed a fivefold minister, whatever their gift

---

[4] For additional info on this topic see the article *When Did the New Testament Start? When Did the Church Begin?* at the FOL site.

may be. For instance, there are pastors in the body of Christ who shepherd a dozen believers and there are pastors who shepherd hundreds or thousands, but they're *both* pastors.

'Official' Ministers and Independent Ministers

It should be pointed out that there are official and independent fivefold ministers in the body of Christ. Official ministers are those who function *within* the structure of a particular camp/sect/denomination. These ministers receive their credentials through schools in these groups and largely function *within* their camp. In most cases they *only* function within their camp. To one degree or another, their allegiance is to their sect and their human overseers thereof, but hopefully to God & the Holy Scriptures first and foremost.

Independent ministers, by contrast, function outside of sectarian tags even if they might get their human credentials through a particular group or via a school that serves Christians from several sects that operate under the banner of, say, Evangelicals. Of course, some genuine independent ministers don't have proper public credentials at all, but neither did Christ or the original apostles; the latter simply *walked with* Jesus Christ and were anointed of God.

Official ministers are generally reliable sources of Christian ministry, depending on how biblically-based their sect is, but they are naturally prone to the flaws of their camp, whatever those might be. In cases where the Scriptures clearly don't agree with a particular doctrine or practice of their sect, they'll likely side with their group above the Scriptures since it's convenient and that's where they get their bread & butter, so to speak, not to mention their position/recognition.

Few official ministers are willing to risk losing these things, although Martin Luther did so when he boldly posted the 95 theses on the Wittenberg Door and eventually split from the Catholics.

Another downside of ministers functioning solely within the framework of a particular sect is that they can become spiritually inbred with the corresponding rigid sectarianism. Their ministry — e.g. their sermons — are prone to cop a "same old, same old" vibe with little freshness. As a result, they can become *un*inspiring.

The strength of independent ministers is that they are less interested in the official doctrines/practices of a particular sect and more interested in what the God-breathed Scriptures actually teach. They can thus shake things up for believers in a positive way. It goes without saying that receiving from independent ministers can be refreshing and invigorating.

Actually, the Word of God and anointed ministers *should* always shake us up in a positive manner (I'm obviously not talking about abusive tactics, like a wicked spirit of condemnation, which sucks the life out of believers). The potential weakness of independent ministers is that their quirks and lack of strong governing structure can lead them astray into dubious doctrines/practices. However, any minister that simply sticks to the rightly-divided Word of God will avoid this pitfall.

You can read important details about official ministers and independent ministers in chapter **10**.

The Fivefold Ministry Gifts are God-Given Gifts or Positions/Offices, Not Titles

The five ministry gifts are just that, *gifts*. They're God-given talents which enable members of the Church to fulfill the leadership position/office in question, small or great. However, they are not personal titles since there is no indication in the Scriptures of any fivefold minister being referred to with such a title, like Apostle Smith or Pastor John.

For instance, while Paul continually acknowledged his office of apostle (Romans 1:1, 1 Corinthians 1:1, 2 Corinthians 1:1, Ephesians 1:1, 1 Timothy 1:1, etc.), he was simply *addressed as* Paul or "brother Paul" (2 Peter 3:15). Meanwhile Peter was called Peter, John was called John and so on (Galatians 2:6-9). This is **the example** set for us in the blueprint of Holy Scripture and is in line with what the Lord instructed regarding titles (Matthew 23:7-11).

In short, the fivefold ministry gifts are not and never were meant to be titles in the Church for ministers. If Paul & the other great fivefold ministers in the New Testament were secure enough in their relationship with God and their calling to be addressed simply by name, so can ministers since that time, including today.

The reason I bring this topic up is because the "title syndrome" can get pretty eye-rolling and it smacks of the flesh since it's obviously centered around ego. For instance, I was at a church dinner where the pastor corrected his own mother for not addressing him with the title of Pastor. Seriously?

It goes without saying that anyone who goes into ministry because they desire subordinates to constantly refer to them as "Pastor," "Reverend," etc. is going into ministry for the wrong reasons.

Speaking of 'reverend,' this word is used once in the King James Bible and only in reference to the Almighty (Psalm 111:9).

That being said, if a fivefold minister wants to insist on a title for those under them in their ministry, that's their call. What's it to me? However, they should not expect believers who know what the Scriptures plainly teach on this topic to do so.[5]

Weddings and Funerals

Interestingly, there are no references in the Bible to ministers officiating weddings or funerals, including pastors. I point this out because some people seem to think that ministry is mostly about performing one or the other. Evidently God didn't get the memo.

This is *not* to say that ministers shouldn't preside over weddings and funerals. After all, who else better to officiate these ceremonies? So for ministers who are led to oversee weddings and funerals, here are some common sense guidelines:

1. Since believers are instructed in the Bible to "Rejoice with those who rejoice and mourn with those who mourn" (Romans 12:15), please rejoice with those who are celebrating a wedding, like Christ did (John 2:1-11), as well as mourn with those who grieve. Be compassionate both publicly and privately. It's a matter of living in harmony with others (Romans 12:16).
2. Since it's the minister's job to "preach the word…in season and out of season" (2 Timothy 4:2), use the occasion of a wedding or funeral to convey truths from the Scriptures as

---

[5] If you desire more scriptural proof on the irrelevance of personal titles in the Church, see this article *Should Ministers Be Addressed with Titles?* at the FOL site.

led of the Spirit. I'm not saying you should have an altar call, just that you can take advantage of the situation to sow God's Word in the lives of others, like the farmer in the Parable of the Sower (Luke 8:5-15). It's a matter of being Christ's ambassador in both joyful settings and somber ones (2 Corinthians 5:20).

3. At a funeral, if the deceased person was a believer you can emphasize the promise of eternal life (John 3:36 & 1 John 5:11-12), which will naturally encourage family & friends (1 Thessalonians 4:13), not to mention be a 'witness' to the unredeemed.

4. In the event that the deceased was not a believer or his/her spiritual condition was uncertain, do not comment on such things for obvious reasons, but rather use the occasion to share the message of Christ with those present.

Let's conclude **Part I** with something that's not often addressed…

Ministers and R&R

Laziness is of the flesh, of course (Matthew 25:26), but some amount of rest & recreation is necessary and healthy, as long as it doesn't become an 'idol' wherein you're mastered by the activity in question (1 Corinthians 6:12). The Bible teaches that there's "a time to weep and a time to **laugh**, a time to mourn and a time to **dance**" (Ecclesiastes 3:4).

Despite the negative things that occur on a regular basis in this fallen world, including in the political realm, Carol & I find something to heartily laugh about every day. As they say, laughter is the best medicine.

It's just as important to get enough rest so that you're able to function on all cylinders, so to speak, especially with regards to the work you do for the Kingdom.

There's a good example of this in Scripture when Christ sent out the disciples to minister from town to town. It goes without saying that ministry can be challenging and draining. When they returned and gave a good report of their activities they all "withdrew by themselves" to the town of Bethsaida (Luke 9:10).

In short, the Lord recognizes the need for ministers to retreat for rest & refreshing after significant ministry endeavors, which naturally protects them from burnout. So never feel guilty about getting healthy rest & recreation. Just keep a sense of balance and remember the saying: *Moderation in all things is the best policy.*

PART II

The Dynamics of Ministers, Ministries and Believers

Now that we know what the fivefold ministry gifts are and how apostles, prophets, evangelists, pastors and teachers differ, let's look at how such ministers and their ministries relate to the body of Christ — believers in general — and vice versa.

Whereas **Part I** set a basic foundation, **Part II** builds upon this base by going into greater detail.

8

The Four Stages of Spiritual Growth

The Bible reveals that there are four stages of spiritual growth with three of the stages pertaining to believers. While fivefold ministers should ideally be in the highest stage of spiritual development, that's not always the case. How is this relevant to our topic? Because servant-leaders can only take you to where they are. They cannot give others what they don't have. Are you following?

STAGE ONE is actually a stage of spiritual darkness where the individual is separate from God and in need of spiritual regeneration. The next three stages apply to the development of the believer who is spiritually reborn in Christ. The Bible refers to these three Christian stages in terms of **childhood**, **youth** and **maturity**, as shown in 1 John 2:9-14. We'll examine this passage shortly.

Too many Christians get stuck in STAGE TWO, which is the institutional stage of spiritual growth wherein believers learn the fundamentals and are dependent upon pastors for their spiritual health. There's nothing wrong with STAGE TWO unless you get stuck there. This chapter will help you to keep growing and not run aground in STAGE TWO.

As you shall see, not only are the Four Stages of spiritual growth scriptural, understanding them is quite enlightening. Grasping them will help you see **where you are at spiritually** and **where you need to go**. It will also help you to **locate where others are at** so you can understand their position and relate to them accordingly, including fivefold ministers, such as pastors.

There are several ways this relates to our topic of fivefold ministry gifts, but here's an obvious one: While you can receive from *any* believer, whether they're further on than you spiritually or not, it's not wise to serve under a minister who is less mature than you spiritually for obvious reasons, unless of course the Holy Spirit leads you to do so. Why? Because the fivefold minister is the servant-**leader** and therefore he or she should naturally be more mature than those following in his/her footsteps.

Now let's examine each specific stage of spiritual growth:

STAGE ONE: Separation from God / Chaos

This is the classic "sinner" stage where the individual is separate from God and therefore in spiritual darkness. At this stage people are in bondage to the flesh — the sinful nature — to one degree or another. Being that people in this stage are separate from God and in spiritual darkness, you could also describe it as moral chaos.

By the way, I'm not saying that people in this stage don't have a spirit, as every human being has a spirit, but rather that their spirit is dead to God and therefore in need of regeneration.[6]

STAGE TWO cannot occur until the individual is enlightened to his or her needy spiritual condition and turns to God via the good news of the gospel, which is called "the message of *reconciliation*" in Scripture (2 Corinthians 5:18-20). This salvation comes through **repentance** and **faith** (Acts 20:21).

STAGE TWO: Institutional / Fundamental

After reconciliation with God, the new believer will naturally join an assembly/ministry/sect. The group's oversight and instruction provide the necessary structure for him or her and (hopefully) the Bible as well. As such, the **chaos** of STAGE ONE transforms into **order** as the organization provides protection & accountability for the convert along with opportunities to learn, participate, serve, grow and eventually lead in some capacity.

STAGE TWO can be described as "fundamental" because those at this level become attached to the rules and doctrines that their organization advocate, which the elders decree to be fundamental to their faith. Not surprisingly, STAGE TWO believers become discombobulated when these fundamentals are threatened, regardless of whether these "fundamentals" are true, false or somewhere in between. As such, those in this stage are "fundamentalists."

STAGE TWO is essentially **Christian boot camp**. It's a stage of spiritual immaturity where the believer is learning and growing.

---

[6] See the article *Human Nature: Spirit, Mind & Body* at the FOL site for details.

It's an immature stage in the sense that the believer is typically *dependent* upon the group to maintain their spiritual status. Just as in military boot camp recruits need their drill instructors and the military institution or they'll revert back to their civilian ways, Christian converts are very dependent on their assemblies/sects and corresponding elders without which they'll likely fall back into STAGE ONE.

Ideally, the new believer will be in STAGE TWO while simultaneously growing in STAGE THREE and STAGE FOUR, as shown here:

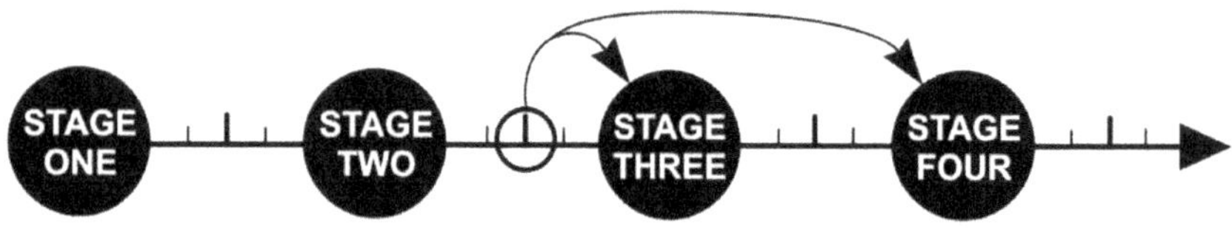

While believers in STAGE TWO should be simultaneously growing in the next two stages, it unfortunately doesn't always happen. Sometimes they get stuck in STAGE TWO, usually because the assembly or sect they hook up with is infected by legalism, which is sterile (counterfeit) Christianity and characterized by rigid sectarianism.

When this occurs, the organization fosters a spirit of dependency in the believer rather than independence, bondage rather than freedom and weakness rather than strength. It's actually spiritual *abuse* and it harms or limits the believer's growth. Abuse, by the way, is the misuse of power.

STAGE THREE: Individual / Seeker

Healthy believers will grow as **individuals** and develop an identity separate from their group. They'll start to question doctrines that don't really gel with the Scriptures or make sense. They'll seek truth — reality — beyond the limitations of their sect and elders, that is, *if* they sense they're in error in one area or another. This is good because error cannot set people free, even if it's disguised as "truth" by one's church or pastor. Only the truth sets free, as Christ taught (John 8:31-32).

Also, as believers develop in STAGE THREE they will cultivate discernment to spiritual abuse and will not tolerate it, which explains why **weak "pastors" try to keep individuals in STAGE TWO**. I put "pastors" in quotes here because *real* pastors passionately desire for believers to grow spiritually.

Now, just because believers in STAGE THREE discover error or abuse in their group it doesn't mean they'll automatically leave. They'll likely stay and do their part to help correct any problems, but this depends on many factors, like: How deeply involved are they in the group? What about their families and close friends? How severe is the error or abuse? What do they discern the Holy Spirit leading them to do? How long have they been trying to help without any appreciable change?

In STAGE THREE believers will find themselves questioning beliefs — possibly even their faith. Because of this, it's a risky and unstable stage in the believer's journey.

I've known people in STAGE TWO who were believers for many years, but as they seemed to transfer to STAGE THREE they totally fall away from God and faith. Usually the signs will be there that this is the way they're heading. Such people failed to "guard their heart as the wellspring of life" (Proverbs 4:23) and allowed things to enter in that took their hearts away from pure devotion to the LORD. Guarding your heart is a matter of wisdom and believers make a big mistake when they allow negative things in that take them away from their "first love" (Mark 4:18-19).

Thankfully, STAGE THREE doesn't end this way for those who *genuinely* seek God and persist rather than use STAGE THREE as an excuse to backtrack to STAGE ONE, as illustrated here:

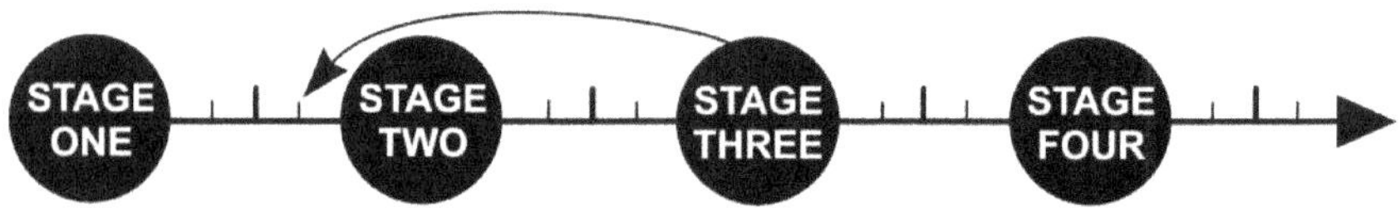

This is an extreme form of what the Bible calls backsliding.

STAGE THREE can be difficult due to its inherent growth pangs just like the teenage years and early 20s can be in the natural, but it's a necessary stage of growth in the believer's spiritual journey. It develops their sense of individuality apart from the group and motivates them to seek out the truth for more certainty and accuracy, not to mention this stage clarifies their objectives.

Without STAGE THREE believers will be stuck in STAGE TWO and they cannot move on to STAGE FOUR.

STAGE FOUR: Knowing God

STAGE FOUR is the stage where believers develop a living *relationship* with God rather than just knowing *about* God or being known *by* God (Galatians 4:9). This is the goal of Christianity and explains why the gospel of Christ is called the "message of reconciliation" (2 Corinthians 5:18-20).

STAGE FOUR is **enlightenment**, **independence** and **strength**. Let's look at all three of these:

STAGE FOUR is **enlightenment** because the believer is in direct communion with God. This communion becomes a 24/7 thing where believers are in constant connection with their Creator. This is what Paul was referring to when he mentioned "praying without ceasing" (1 Thessalonians 5:17). Enlightenment in this manner includes the constant awareness of God's presence via the Holy Spirit and also the awesomeness, beauty and mystery of actually knowing the LORD.

Those stuck in STAGE TWO, by contrast, only have an inkling of this and basically view God as a big cop in the sky (please notice I specified those *stuck in* STAGE TWO). This is an *outward* perspective of God and it's frankly an Old Testament mentality. The New Testament emphasizes the believer's spiritual regeneration and the indwelling empowerment of the Holy Spirit — God is *within us!* See Titus 3:5, 1 Corinthians 3:16 and Ephesians 1:19.

STAGE FOUR is **independence** from bondage to the error and corruption that often comes with the institution of STAGE TWO. Please read that again and chew on it. This isn't to say that the assembly/sect/pastors that believers are hooked up with in STAGE TWO are *always* bad or that they're all bad — not at all — they're usually good and definitely necessary, but error and abuse come with the territory of people and groups, even Christian churches and sects. Are you following?

Furthermore, STAGE FOUR is **independence** from the uncertainty of STAGE THREE. How so? In STAGE FOUR believers know God personally. They've "tasted and seen that the LORD is good" (Psalm 34:8). As such, it's impossible for someone to convince them that God doesn't exist because they personally walk with the LORD.

This isn't to say, of course, that believers in STAGE FOUR are exempt from falling from faith, only that it's much harder for them to fall than those in STAGE TWO or THREE. Why? Because they're actually walking with God 24/7.

This combination of enlightenment and independence makes for **strong** believers. They're spiritually mature. These are people who know God and increasingly know their calling. They don't just sacrifice 10% of their finances as a tithe since their whole lives are "living sacrifices" when they wake up in the morning (Romans 12:1). Because they discern and fulfill God's will on both minor and major levels they become a threat to the enemy's kingdom, which naturally draws attack. This includes opposition from people at lower stages of spiritual growth, including quasi-believers and religious legalists, like the Pharisees.

Furthermore, those in STAGE FOUR become increasingly **independent** of the need of others in order to stay tight with God and fulfill their calling. What I'm saying is that believers in STAGE TWO and even THREE will fall back into STAGE ONE without the service, support and encouragement of fellow believers, particularly in the context of church services, but those firmly walking in STAGE FOUR don't need others to walk free of the pitfalls of the flesh and legalism. They don't need others to motivate them to spiritual disciplines, like prayer, study, worship, fasting, service, etc.

Don't get me wrong here, Paul was encouraged and blessed by other believers, as every Christian should be, but Paul performed spiritual disciplines and fulfilled his calling without people over him compelling him to do so. It goes without saying that every believer should aspire to this level of spirituality. The ones who don't are not spiritually mature.

By the way, I'm not saying that believers in STAGE FOUR shouldn't attend assembly services. Going to healthy church gatherings as led of the Spirit is always good, regardless of where you're at spiritually. But those in STAGE FOUR will often lead their own ministries within other ministries or start their own, whether within an existing camp or otherwise. (It depends on if they're an "official" minister or an independent minister, which we'll look at in chapter **10**).

In light of all this, STAGE FOUR is a stage of **strength**. But there is a downside: "Higher levels bigger devils." Thankfully, those in STAGE FOUR can handle the increased attacks and their intensity because, again, they're tight with the LORD.

A good scriptural example is Paul who endured great persecutions while he traveled the eastern Mediterranean area starting numerous churches and overseeing them. He was trailblazing and trailblazers are usually very independent, spiritually speaking. Check out Paul's list of persecutions in 2 Corinthians 11:23-28; it's incredible. Someone in STAGE TWO or STAGE THREE could never endure such hardships without falling away, but those in the higher levels of STAGE FOUR can, just as Paul did.

Getting Stuck in STAGE TWO

As already noted, believers in STAGE TWO should simultaneously be growing in STAGE THREE and FOUR. In other words, as believers grow in the realm of **Christian community** (STAGE TWO), they should also be growing as an **individual** (STAGE THREE) and in their **relationship with God** (STAGE FOUR). Healthy believers always have a finger, hand or foot in the next stage (or the next level of the stage they're in). The Bible refers to this maturation from one level to the next as going "from strength to strength" or "glory to glory" (Psalm 84:5,7 & 2 Corinthians 3:18).

But what of those who get stuck in STAGE TWO? These are people who fail to develop spiritually as individuals and in relationship with their Creator. Instead, the institution they are involved with — their assembly and its camp — replaces both. This isn't good because, in essence, the institution itself takes the place of God. They become "sheeple" — mindless automatons dedicated to perpetuating the machine of the institution, their "god."

This explains why those stuck in STAGE TWO typically become rigid sectarians who eye outsiders suspiciously and get irate when someone merely questions the legitimacy of a rule and doctrine of their group. Why is this so? Because the institution has taken the place of the LORD. You see this with cults like the Jehovah's False Witnesses. It's really a form of idolatry.

Non-Christian Substitutions

There are obvious secular *substitutions* to STAGE TWO. Prison is a good example. Individuals in the lower levels of STAGE ONE inevitably break the law because of their darkened spiritual condition, which predictably lands them in jail or prison. Their new environment provides the parameters and order they need to escape the chaos of STAGE ONE, but as soon as they're released back into the public they revert back to STAGE ONE because they can't handle the freedom. They're ***dependent* on the institution** to keep them from iniquity, at least outwardly.

Religious and non-religious institutions are also substitutes, like Sciencefictionology, Mormonism, TM, rehabs, psyche wards, 12-step programs, martial arts programs and a gazillion others. They're not all bad, of course, at least as far as helping the individual escape the darkness and chaos of STAGE ONE, but all such disciplines pale in comparison to the effectiveness of genuine Christianity (as opposed to sterile, religious "Christianity") because true Christianity solves humanity's root problem — the condition of spiritual death and separation from God.

The family can also be a substitute (and in the believer's life it plays an accessory role). For instance, individuals who grow up in strong families that have a lot of love, order and discipline essentially grow up without experiencing the darkness and chaos of STAGE ONE. They were, in essence, born into STAGE TWO.

This is normally a good thing and those with healthy families like this should be praising the Lord that they largely skipped STAGE ONE. This only becomes a problem if the individual becomes arrogant (spoiled) due to his or her good fortune, which is a sure slide into STAGE ONE, keeping in mind that arrogance — a superiority complex — is sin *numero uno* in God's eyes. This brings up an important point…

STAGE FOUR Believers are HUMBLE

Since STAGE FOUR believers are at the highest stage of spiritual growth (although not necessarily the highest *level*, as there are levels within each stage), it's easy to assume that they'd be arrogant, but this isn't the case at all. People who genuinely know the LORD are extremely humble because "God resists the proud, but gives his favor to the humble" (James 4:6 & 1 Peter 5:5). As such, only the humble can get close to God. The LORD only knows arrogant people "from afar" (Psalm 138:6).

If you know domineering Christians who love to bloviate and abuse, they're not in STAGE FOUR. They're in STAGE TWO or THREE with their heads in STAGE ONE. See chapters **13** and **14** for details.

John's References to the Four Stages

An excellent biblical reference to the Four Stages of spiritual growth can be observed in this passage:

> **Anyone who claims to be in the light but hates a brother or sister is still <u>in the darkness</u>.** [10]**Anyone who loves their brother and sister lives in the light, and there is nothing in them to make them stumble.** [11] **But anyone who hates a brother or sister is <u>in the darkness</u> and walks around <u>in the darkness</u>. They do not know where they are going, because the darkness has blinded them.**
>
> [12] **I am writing to you, dear <u>children</u>, because your sins have been forgiven on account of his name.**

¹³ I am writing to you, <u>fathers</u>,

    because you know him who is from the beginning.

I am writing to you, <u>young men</u>,

    because you have overcome the evil one.

¹⁴ I write to you, dear <u>children</u>,

    because you know the Father.

I write to you, <u>fathers</u>,

    because you know him who is from the beginning.

I write to you, <u>young men</u>,

    because you are strong,

    and the word of God lives in you,

    and you have overcome the evil one.

1 John 2:9-14

John wasn't being literal with his references to "children," "young men" and "fathers," but rather figurative. We know this for several reasons:

1. Literal children wouldn't even read his epistle and wouldn't understand it if someone read it to them.

2. Not all mature believers reading his epistle (then or now) would be literal fathers — Paul's a good example — but all spiritually mature believers are *spiritual* fathers and mothers.

3. Elsewhere when Paul *literally* referred to segments of the congregation by the Spirit he did so in a more universal manner, as shown in Colossians 3:18-24 (i.e. wives, husbands, children, fathers and slaves).

4. John's references to "children," "young men" and "fathers" simply fits the Four Stage model, particularly since he referred to STAGE ONE three times in the previous three verses.

Hence the references to the Four Stages in this passage can be summed up as follows:

- "In the darkness" refers to the **spiritual darkness** of STAGE ONE where an unbeliever is separate from the light of God because his or her spirit is dead to the LORD.
- "Children" is a reference to the **boot camp fundamentalism** of STAGE TWO wherein the believer establishes a foundation. Unfortunately, too many Christians get stuck in this stage and never grow beyond it. They live and die as spiritual children.
- "Young men" refers to the **growing individualism and sense of freedom and adulthood** of STAGE THREE.
- "Fathers" is a reference to the **maturity and independence** of STAGE FOUR where believers naturally propagate.

Since there's neither male nor female in Christ (Galatians 3:28) we can broaden the terms for STAGE TWO, THREE and FOUR as such: children, young people and parents or, better yet, **childhood, youth** and **maturity**. Let's fit these into our Four Stages diagram:

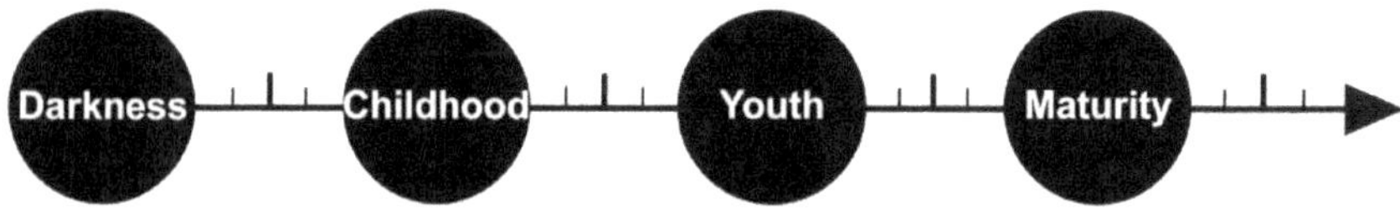

There are awesome pastors out there, praise the Lord, but some are weak — or even counterfeits — in that they encourage the pastoral *dependency* of STAGE TWO ("children") and are threatened by those believers trying to move into the next two stages. Instead of thinking in terms of apprehending new disciples — converts — they think in terms of "holding on" to their current fold by intentionally keeping them in the dependent stage of STAGE TWO.

They don't want to 'lose' them, not realizing that 'losing them' is the best thing for them because these believers would grow up spiritually, becoming "young men" (STAGE THREE) and "fathers" (STAGE FOUR). As a minister I know put it:

> *My job is to become unnecessary in the life of the believer.*

9

Shepherds Naturally Look for Sheep to Shepherd

There's something everyone should know about pastors and overseers in general, including apostles. We saw in chapter **5** that the Greek word for 'pastor' is *poimén (poy-MAYN)*, which literally means "shepherd" and figuratively refers to "a person the Lord raises up to *care for* the well-being of God's flock." This is the call of all genuine pastors and so they're naturally on the lookout for 'sheep' who *need* shepherding.

The less shepherding a believer requires — i.e. care, feeding and supervision — the less interested the pastor will be in him or her. The exception would be mature believers who can assist the pastor in shepherding the sheep, which would be subordinate pastors. If you don't qualify for either of these the pastor in question won't likely be very interested in you. There's nothing wrong with this because it's just the way it is.

I point this out for those who have grown beyond STAGE TWO and are well into STAGE THREE or the early levels of STAGE

FOUR.[7] Unless you are called to a subordinate pastoral or supportive position in a fellowship — including elder, counselor, deacon or financial supporter — the pastor simply won't be interested in you.

Don't be offended in these cases because the pastor *shouldn't* be interested in you. People at your level of spiritual growth don't need the pastor, generally speaking, and pastors are only interested in those who need their services or are called to support their ministries, as detailed. The ultimate purpose of pastors is to shepherd believers to the point where they no longer require the shepherding of a pastor.

I was well into STAGE THREE and the early levels of STAGE FOUR when I noticed that pastors at churches weren't very interested in me when I was looking for a local fellowship. I should say "we" because my wife, Carol, was with me, but I'll keep this on a personal level. They'd essentially eye me up and down to discern where I was at spiritually. When they discerned that I didn't need them in order to walk closely with the LORD they didn't want much to do with me.

Instead of becoming offended and badmouthing them — which are immature signs of STAGE ONE or TWO — I prayed for them and continued to seek the Lord's will for my life, which ultimately led to the birth of Fountain of Life Teaching Ministry and all that goes with it.

I encourage you to do the same if you experience this in your walk. Don't revile pastors for being what they are — pastors. Don't revile overseers for being what they are — overseers. Instead,

---

[7] See the previous chapter if you're unfamiliar with the Four Stages of spiritual growth.

praise God that you no longer need them and are free to move on to new levels in the spirit. If you're going to be mad at anyone be mad at yourself for trying to stay in the childhood or youth stage of Christianity when you've outgrown both.

This is not to say, by the way, that believers can't be blessed by the ministries of pastors who don't want them in their fellowships. You can receive from *anyone* who rightly divides God's Word and has worthy insights. Eat the meat and spit out the bones or, as the Bible puts it: "Test everything. Hold on to the good" (1 Thessalonians 5:21).

10

Official Ministers and Independent Ministers

A prophet is someone who proposes to speak for the LORD and therefore represents God. This is also true of a New Testament minister. A good example from the Bible is Paul (Ephesians 6:19-20).[8] In the Old Testament we observe two kinds of prophets:

1. **Official prophets** who served on the king's court wherein they advised the kings of Israel or Judah, such as Nathan during David's reign (2 Samuel 7:1-17, 12:1-14 & 1 Kings 1:22-23).
2. **Independent prophets** who functioned outside the official sanction of the king, like Elijah, who opposed Ahab, the king of Israel (1 Kings 18:16-21).

Both types are good and necessary but — as with anything — each *can* be corrupted. When corruption enters the picture, abuse is always nearby.

---

[8] It could be argued of course that *all* spiritually-reborn believers represent the LORD as "ambassadors of Christ" (2 Corinthians 5:17-20), which is why we have to watch our 'witness' — the example we set in everyday life.

The potential pitfall for official prophets is that they can easily become "yes men" or "yes women" in an effort to maintain their position and recognition. The obvious challenge for independent prophets is their immediate lack of human accountability and potential for unorthodox positions, meaning *unbiblical* teachings.

A good example of the former would be the 400 "official" prophets of Israel that righteous Jehoshaphat, king of Judah, recognized as dubious:

> **But Jehoshaphat also said to the king of Israel, "First seek the counsel of the Lord."**
>
> **⁶ So <u>the king of Israel brought together the prophets</u>—about four hundred men—and asked them, "Shall I go to war against Ramoth Gilead, or shall I refrain?"**
>
> **"Go," they answered, "for the Lord will give it into the king's hand."**
>
> **⁷ But Jehoshaphat asked, "<u>Is there no longer a prophet of the Lord here whom we can inquire of</u>?"**
>
> **1 Kings 22:5-7**

Jehoshaphat was the upright monarch of Judah whereas Ahab was the wicked king of Israel, although it should be noted that Ahab had a sincere season of repentance around this particular time (1 Kings 21:25-29). Whatever the case, it's clear that Jehoshaphat didn't trust these 400 "official" prophets who served Ahab. He discerned that they were worthless "yes men." So he inquired of Ahab:

…"Is there no longer a prophet <u>of the Lord</u> here whom we can inquire of?"

⁸ The king of Israel answered Jehoshaphat, "There is still <u>one prophet</u> through whom we can inquire of the Lord, but I hate him because he never prophesies anything good about me, but always bad. He is <u>Micaiah</u> son of Imlah."

"The king should not say such a thing," Jehoshaphat replied.

⁹ So the king of Israel called one of his officials and said, "Bring Micaiah son of Imlah at once."

1 Kings 22:7-9

Micaiah *(mih-CAY-ah)* was an independent prophet who was unknown to the king of Judah and disregarded by Ahab because he refused to tickle the king's ears with untruths. Notice how Micaiah responds to the herald who was sent to get him:

The messenger who had gone to summon Micaiah said to him, "Look, <u>the other prophets without exception are predicting success for the king. Let your word agree with theirs</u>, and speak favorably."

¹⁴ But Micaiah said, "As surely as the Lord lives, <u>I can tell him only what the Lord tells me</u>."

1 Kings 22:13-14

As you can see, the envoy *pressured* this independent prophet to agree with the words of Ahab's numerous official prophets, but Micaiah nobly stressed that he could only convey what the LORD gave him to say. Observe what happens next:

> **When he arrived, the king asked him, "Micaiah, shall we go to war against Ramoth Gilead, or not?"**
>
> **"Attack and be victorious," he answered, "for the LORD will give it into the king's hand."**
>
> **1 Kings 22:15**

Micaiah was implementing sarcasm here, amusingly mimicking Ahab's 400 "official" prophets. He then proceeded to tell Ahab and Jehoshaphat the truth, which you can look up yourself.

Uriah was the high priest during the reign of wicked Ahaz, king of Judah. He is another sad example of an official minister who weakly just goes with the flow in order to maintain his position and keep bread & butter on the table. King Ahaz went to Damascus to meet the king of Assyria wherein he noticed an altar to Asshur (aka Assur), the false god worshiped by the Assyrians. He thus sent Uriah in Jerusalem sketches of the pagan altar and corresponding instructions concerning idolatrous worship. The account culminates with this sad statement: "and Uriah the Priest did just as King Ahaz had ordered" (2 Kings 16:10-16).

Keep in mind that Uriah was *supposed* to be the high priest of the LORD and that the previous king of Judah was righteous, as well as the following king (the father and son of Ahaz respectively). Wouldn't you think that the head priest closest to the throne would defend staying faithful to Yahweh and adamantly object to gross pagan idolatry in God's Temple? Not in this case.

Uriah might have been an "official" minister of the LORD, but obviously not in his heart or practice. We see similar "official" ministers today in various compromised sects and assemblies. Whatever dubious doctrines & practices are approved by the authorities of their sect they just weakly go with the flow.

In contrast to Ahab's 400 prophets and Uriah the high priest, Nathan is an example of an official prophet who refused to become a pathetic "yes man." He boldly spoke the truth and confronted error when applicable, come what may (2 Samuel 12:1-14).

As noted above, Elijah and Micaiah are good examples of righteous independent prophets, as is Jeremiah (Jeremiah 1:17-19). The unnamed "man of God" who rebuked Eli, the High Priest at Shiloh, is another good example (1 Samuel 2:27-36). Keep in mind that Eli was a descendant of Aaron and so his position was of that magnitude, not to mention he "judged" Israel for 40 years, meaning he led the nation (1 Samuel 4:18). In short, Eli fulfilled the office of both priest and judge of Israel during that time.

All the official ministers in Israel would've technically been under Eli and would've understandably been leery about confronting & correcting someone of such stature. Yet this independent "man of God" didn't allow Eli's great position to prevent him from fulfilling God's instruction. This is one of the reasons we need independent ministers.

An example of an independent prophet becoming corrupt is the nameless old prophet who lied to a younger prophet simply referred to as a "man of God." He lied about an angel supposedly visiting him and giving him instructions which deviated from the LORD's personal instructions to the younger prophet (1 Kings 13). Foolishly believing the older prophet's lie and disregarding the Lord's direct instructions resulted in his death (verses 18-25).

Official Ministers and Independent Ministers in the New Testament Era

The history of Israel and the patriarchs in the Old Testament serve as ***examples*** to us, the worldwide Church (Romans 15:4 & 1 Corinthians 10:11). God's kingdom reigned on Earth in the Old Testament via the *physical* nation of Israel whereas God's kingdom reigns on Earth in the New Testament period thru the *spiritual* nation of the Church (1 Peter 2:9). We're currently living in the New Testament era, of course.

Israel was led by kings, priests, judges and prophets (Jeremiah 2:26) while the Church is led by apostles, prophets, evangelists, pastors and teachers, which means fivefold ministers (Ephesians 4:11-13). 'Minister' means "servant," of course, so the Church is led by *servant*-leaders.

Just as Israel had official prophets and independent prophets, so the Church has official ministers and independent ministers. Official ministers in the Church are those who operate within the frame of a specific group. These ministers obtain their credentials via schools in these organizations and usually function exclusively *within* the sect. In most cases they *only* function within their group. Their loyalty is naturally to their camp, but hopefully to God & the Holy Scriptures above all.

Independent ministers, however, operate outside of sectarian labels even if they might get their human qualifications through a particular group or a seminary that serves believers from myriad organizations. Evangelical or Charismatic colleges are good examples. Of course, some genuine independent ministers don't have appropriate credentials at all, yet neither did Christ or the apostles. The apostles simply *walked with* the Lord and were empowered of the Spirit.

I personally was ordained at a special service in 2006 and received a diploma from a reputable Bible college in 2010. When I got these credentials I put 'em under my bed and continued to do what I was already doing in service of the Lord. Actually, they're displayed on my wall; I'm just making a point.

Just as the physical nation of Israel was split into sects after Solomon's reign, specifically Judah and the Northern Kingdom of Israel (1 Kings 12) — and, for a brief period, Benjamin separated to essentially (and foolishly) fight for homosexual rights (Judges 19-21) — so the spiritual nation of the worldwide Church is split up into sects, some good, some bad and many somewhere in between.

Even if you're part of a particular sect — and there's nothing wrong with that if it's where the Lord leads you to grow/serve — it's best to strive to be as non-sectarian as possible.[9] Where and how you function & serve in the body of Christ is determined by your stage of spiritual growth (as detailed in chapter **8**), as well as the Lord's calling and the Holy Spirit's leading.

A Scriptural Example of an Independent Servant of Christ

An example of an independent minister can be seen on this occasion (observed from two different accounts):

---

[9] For details see the article at the FOL site *Sectarianism — What is It? What's Wrong with It?*

> "Master," said John, "we saw someone driving out demons in your name and we tried to stop him, <u>because he is not one of us</u>."
> ⁵⁰ "<u>Do not stop him</u>," Jesus said, "for <u>whoever is not against you is for you</u>."
>
> **Luke 9:49-50**

> "Teacher," said John, "we saw someone driving out demons in your name and we told him to stop, <u>because he was not one of us</u>."
> ³⁹ "<u>Do not stop him</u>," Jesus said. "For no one who does a miracle in my name can in the next moment say anything bad about me, ⁴⁰ for <u>whoever is not against us is for us</u>.
>
> **Mark 9:38-40**

At this particular time Christ & the disciples represented the only "sect" of Christianity on Earth, but John noticed someone operating *outside* of their "sect," driving out evil spirits from demon-oppressed people. John was growing in the Lord, of course, yet he was obviously still spiritually *immature,* which can be seen in his religious reaction to an independent disciple boldly carrying out the work of Christ (Acts 10:38). John wanted to stop the man simply because he wasn't "one of them"; in other words, the man served God *outside* of John's group and so he instinctively objected.

This is the spirit of sectarianism, which is a work of the flesh and a form of religious legalism. Christian legalism is counterfeit spirituality. People who function according to rigid sectarianism, like John here, are in STAGE TWO spiritual growth; and an early level at that. Yet notice that the Lord had no issue with this independent minister on the grounds of "whoever is not against us is for us."

Why is this account in the New Testament, *twice?* To show us that God has zero problem with believers taking the initiative and doing the work of the LORD independent of the in-vogue sect, whatever that might be. Please note that Christ did *not* say, "Yes, he must be discouraged and stopped immediately — he is not accountable!"

We have to get away from this childish idea that, unless believers have official sanction from a certain sect, they can't do anything legitimate for the kingdom of God and they're not worthy of ministering and receiving from. Christian servant-leaders — whether apostles, prophets, evangelists, pastors or teachers — are *not* limited to a man-made religious box! (Which is *not* to say that genuine Christian sects or camps are all "man-made religious boxes," just that they *can* be).

Strengths & Weaknesses of Official Ministers and Independent Ministers

Assuming the group in question strives to be Bible-believing and Bible-teaching, official ministers are reliable sources of Christian ministry, but they're naturally prone to the imperfections of their organization, whatever those might be. In cases where God's Word clearly doesn't support a particular doctrine or practice of their camp, they'll likely side with their sect above the Scriptures since it's expedient and that's where they get their financial support, not to mention their position & prestige.

Not many official ministers are willing to risk losing such things, although Martin Luther did when he boldly posted the 95 theses on the Wittenberg Door and later left the Catholic sect.[10]

---

[10] I'm well aware of the several unbiblical doctrines/practices of Catholics, which are detailed at the FOL site in the article *Roman Catholicism – Is it the*

Another shortcoming of ministers functioning exclusively within the parameters of a certain group is that they can become spiritually inbred with the matching staunch sectarianism. Their ministry deeds — such as their sermons — are prone to cop a "same old, same old" air with little freshness. Unsurprisingly, they can become *un*inspiring.

The strength of independent ministers is that they're less interested in the official doctrines/practices of a particular sect and more interested in what the God-breathed Scriptures actually teach. They can shake things up for believers in a positive way. Needless to say, receiving from independent ministers can be refreshing and stimulating.

Actually, anointed ministers and the corresponding Word of God *should* always rattle our cages in an inspiring way (I'm not referring to abusive actions, like a fleshly spirit of condo, which drains the life out of people). The potential weakness of such ministers is that their quirks and lack of immediate accountability can possibly steer them astray into questionable teachings or practices. However, any minister that remains devoted to the rightly-divided Word of God will elude this failing.

Diotrephes *(dye-OT-rah-feez)* was a pastor within John the apostle's circuit of fellowships. He clearly wanted to become more independent in ministry, which is wonderful, but he started walking in the flesh to achieve this goal, which *isn't* good. Notice what John frankly said about him, led of the Spirit:

"Original Church"? Yet I've met genuine believers who serve the LORD under that particular sectarian tag. As such, while there's certainly a place for speaking the truth in (tough) love, it's wise to focus on being pro-Jesus Christ as opposed to being doggedly anti-Catholic.

> **I wrote to the church, but Diotrephes, who loves to be first, <u>will have nothing to do with us.</u> [10] So if I come, I will call attention to what he is doing, <u>gossiping maliciously about us.</u> Not satisfied with that, <u>he refuses to welcome the brothers.</u> He also stops those who want to do so and <u>puts them out of the church.</u>**
>
> **3 John 1:9-10**

Diotrephes had to be the head pastor of the assembly. After all, who else would have the authority to prevent leaders of John's stature from coming and ministering? Who else has the power to excommunicate but the pastor? Unfortunately, in Diotrephes' desire to become more independent in ministry, he took a grossly carnal turn — slandering leaders and unjustly excommunicating believers. We'll look at this in more detail in chapter **14**.

Christ was an Independent Minister

For the record, Jesus was an independent minister. Sure, he was a Judaic believer who regularly attended synagogue, but he didn't **identify** with any of the various Hebrew factions of the 1st Century: Pharisees, Sadducees, Herodians, Essenes, Zealots, etc. Being independent and devoted to God & the Scriptures first and foremost, Christ wasn't biased based around sectarian allegiances.

Interestingly, while he warned his listeners about the corruption of the Teachers of the Law, he didn't hesitate to commend one such teacher when appropriate (compare Mark 12:38-40 and Mark 12:28-34). In other words, just because a person belonged to a group he denounced, the Messiah was able to give merit where it was due. We should do the same.

Likewise, independent ministers today are decidedly Christian, but they don't necessarily identify with a specific group, like the Assemblies of God, Baptist, Reformed, Nazarene, Church of Christ, Word of Faith, Lutheran, Methodist, Episcopal, Catholic and so forth. There are much smaller sects in most local areas. This is not to say that independent ministers won't minister within the framework of any of these groups. They can and do. It's just that they refuse to allow the doctrines/practices of these groups to inhibit their service in the Lord.

When official ministers allow independent ministers to serve at one of their services they usually have to get the permission of the higher authorities of their particular sect. If not, there can be repercussions. For instance, the Assemblies of God require pastors to obtain permission to allow ministers outside of their camp to minister at a service.

Years ago a Nazarene pastor I know allowed an independent prophet to minister at several services in his assembly, but this prophet was a Charismatic, i.e. he believed and functioned in the gifts of the Spirit (1 Corinthians 12:1-11). Apparently that's a no-no for Nazarenes because the pastor swiftly got kicked out of his denomination and had to move to Nova Scotia to pastor another fellowship.

What about the "Lone Wolf"?

I've been involved with sects in which the leaders write off independent ministers as "lone wolves," obviously in order to keep their congregants from receiving from them. While there are certainly dubious independent 'ministers' who could be labeled "lone wolves" since they lack fruit of the spirit and deviate from the rightly-divided Word of God (Matthew 7:15-23), it's wrong to use this as an excuse to dismiss all independent ministers since they are strategic in the body of Christ, as already explained.

It goes without saying that, whilst it's understandable that pastors naturally want to protect growing believers in their assemblies, it's wrong to slander legitimate ministers who function independently of an official sect.

Besides, the "lone wolf" argument can be turned around on those who dubiously employ it. Wolves, after all, hunt in *packs*. Likewise wolves in the ministry usually function within the pack of a sect. A glaring example from the scriptures is Judas, who was one of Christ's original twelve disciples. Then there are the false apostles who slandered Paul to the believers at Corinth, an assembly he pioneered (2 Corinthians 11).

Who Should You Receive from—Official Ministers or Independent Ministers?

I remember an occasion where I went to the hospital to visit someone. It was in the heat of the summer and so I naturally wore shorts, sandals and a t-shirt (with cut-off sleeves). By happenstance, the woman in the elevator with me was clearly a member of some religious sect in light of her apparel. Official ministers tend to wear some outward sign that they're a minister, like a clerical collar; not always, but more so than independent ministers. The latter tend to take the more casual approach in order to fit in à la 1 Corinthians 9:19-23. Despite our polar opposite approaches, both of us were at the hospital *for the very same reason*, to visit the sick and minister accordingly.

So who do you receive from — official ministers or independent ones? Why not **both** since the Bible includes each type in the Old and New Testaments? Learn to "eat the meat and spit out the bones," whether you're receiving from an official minister or an independent one. This is a modern rephrasing of something encouraged in the New Testament (1 Thessalonians 5:19-21).

Be aware of the strengths and potential weaknesses of both official and independent prophets. Reject the problematic or dubious, but receive the good. If you're not sure something is scriptural put it on the back burner, so to speak, until you acquire more detailed information in order to draw a proper conclusion.

But don't just blindly accept whatever your camp/sect/assembly *says* is true, because it might not be. Keep in mind that all fivefold ministers are human beings with individual quirks. All of them have a downside, *all* of them. There's no such thing as a perfect minister, just like there's no such thing as a perfect church/camp/sect.

However, the minister should be free of sin as a lifestyle and it's important that they show evidence of the fruit of the spirit on a consistent basis (Matthew 7:15-23 & Galatians 5:19-23). They must be completely freed-up from major sin and, when they miss it in smaller areas, they should be humble enough to admit it and spiritual enough to quickly 'fess up, receive forgiveness, and move on (1 John 1:8-9).

If you sense in a minister an abusive, accusatory or rigidly legalistic spirit with little evidence of fruit of the spirit, **head to the hills**, whether it's an official minister or an independent one. This is what Christ instructed us to do (Matthew 15:14). Since pride is sin *numero uno*, **arrogance is the worst indicator**. I'm talking about a pompous, boastful, condescending spirit that refuses to ever admit they're wrong and loves to manipulate.

The starkest evidence of arrogance is when a supposed minister insists that only he/she and their particular group is the "one true church" and every minister/assembly *outside* their group is false. These types are quick to call anyone a "false teacher" who happens to disagree with their conclusions on any jot or tittle of Scripture. Of course they justify such rash pomposity under the guise of "spiritual boldness." It's both eye-rolling and cult-ish.

Needless to say, if you come across one of these types flee for your spiritual welfare. Even if they're right on a particular issue, so what? *Everyone* is right about *something.* Their gross arrogance tells you everything you need to know. *Leave them* (Matthew 15:14).

Lastly, the doctrines (teachings) a minister teaches/preaches should be as biblical as possible because the Holy Scriptures are the LORD's blueprint for authentic Christian doctrine and practice (1 Corinthians 4:6 & 2 Timothy 3:16-17). Ministers should be held accountable to what God's Word teaches based on sound hermeneutics. We'll look at accountability further in chapter **18**.

11

Should You "Obey" Your Spiritual Leaders?

There's one verse in the Bible where it suggests that believers are to "obey" their spiritual leaders:

> **Obey your leaders and submit to their authority. They keep watch over you as those who must give an account. Obey them so that their work will be a joy, not a burden, for that would be of no advantage to you."**
>
> **Hebrews 13:17**

The verse instructs us to "obey" those who are over us in the Lord and "submit to their authority." Does this mean to obey and submit in the absolute sense? If your spiritual leaders told you to jump off the roof of a building, should you do it? Of course not. If they instructed you to do something immoral, like commit adultery or fornication, should you do it? Clearly not. So these instructions have obvious parameters or limitations. Such limitations can be observed throughout the rest of the New Testament.

The exhortation here to submit to spiritual leaders and obey them is akin to other appeals in the Epistles for wives to submit to husbands, children to obey parents and believers to submit to governing authorities (Ephesians 5:22-6:9 & Romans 13:1-6). Such instructions are only applicable when the authority gives good or neutral instructions. Otherwise "we must obey God rather than human beings" (Acts 5:29).

One important guideline of Bible interpretation is that we must "interpret Scripture with Scripture," meaning our interpretation of a passage has to gel with what the rest of Scripture teaches on that topic, as long as it's relevant (for instance, dietary laws for Hebrews under the Old Covenant are decidedly *irrelevant* to New Testament believers as observed in Colossians 2:16-17 & Mark 7:19).

You see, the Bible itself is the ultimate **context** of every passage and, therefore, every passage must be interpreted **within** that context, not to mention its more immediate context, that is, the book/chapter/verses in question. Clearer and more detailed passages obviously trump the more ambiguous and sketchy ones. This paves the way for *balance* and keeps believers from taking one or two passages and going to extremes.

Consider the above verse, Hebrews 13:17. Authoritarian pastors could take it and implement a spirit of domination over their congregants. For example, they could say: "As a believer you are obligated to obey God's Word and God's Word says that you *must* submit to me and obey me." They might say it in a more subtle manner but, regardless, this fosters an unhealthy dictatorial environment.

We know for a fact that the passage doesn't give ministers a license to be authoritarian because 1 Peter 5:1-4 plainly states that spiritual leaders are to "serve" and *not* "lord it over" believers, as covered in chapter **5**. Moreover, Christ repeatedly rebuked the arrogance of the religious leaders of 1st Century Israel. Luke 11 and Matthew 23 contain good examples.

Notice what Jesus plainly taught about Christian leadership to his 12 disciples:

> **"You know that the rulers of the Gentiles <u>lord it over them</u>, and their high officials <u>exercise authority over them</u>.** [26] **<u>Not so with you</u>. Instead, <u>whoever wants to become great among you must be your servant</u>,** [27] **and <u>whoever wants to be first must be your slave</u> —** [28] **just as the Son of Man did not come to be served, but to serve, and to give his life as a ransom for many."**
>
> **Matthew 20:25-28**

This doesn't mean, of course, that Christian leaders are to be spineless milksops; Christ, Peter, Paul and John were anything but that, yet it does reveal the style of leadership believers are to have — an attitude of a servant or slave. Do servants or slaves bully those they serve? Do they "exercise authority" with a dictatorial, intimidating air? Obviously not. The Messiah taught that Christian leaders are not to be like this, period.

Furthermore, beware of a spirit of condemnation — aka "condo" — wherein the minister tends to put believers down and tries to shame them into obedience. We saw in chapter **1** that the authority ministers possess is for **building believers up** and *not* tearing them down. Paul stressed this when he detailed the purpose of all fivefold ministers: "to prepare God's people for works of service, so that the body of Christ may be **built up**." (We'll look at this further in chapter **13**).

Of course this doesn't negate the necessity of righteous correction when appropriate (Matthew 18:15-17 & Proverbs 27:5), keeping in mind that correction works *both* ways (in other words, if the pastor or any other spiritual mentor is walking in sin or teaching false doctrine *they* need to be corrected).

With this understanding, never feel obligated to submit to or obey ministers who have an arrogant, domineering bearing. If you do, I guarantee you'll be abused in some manner down the road.

As for those who have proven their godly character and sound doctrine via rightly dividing the Scriptures (as opposed to just weakly parroting whatever their sect/camp *claims* is true doctrine), please submit to them so that their work will be a joy and not a burden. Hold them in the highest regard in love, assuming they're diligent and not lazy (1 Thessalonians 5:12-13). After all, if their work is a joy they'll obviously serve better and you'll be blessed because of it. This is just common sense.

Submit to their vision for the local assembly and worldwide Church; do your part to help it manifest. If you can't do this, please leave and find a fellowship with whose vision you can agree. After all, two opposing visions naturally create **di-vision**.

As far as *obeying* spiritual authorities goes, we've already established that this does not mean to obey them in an absolute sense. The Greek word translated as "obey" in Hebrews 13:17 is *peithó (PAI-thoh)*, which means **to be persuaded by what is trustworthy**. For instance, the Lord *persuades* the yielded believer to be confident in the preferred-will of God. This involves obedience, yes, but it is the result of God's persuasion through **1.** the proper instruction/interpretation of Holy Scripture and **2.** the leading of the Spirit.

This understanding of *peithó* can be observed in Galatians 5:10 in which the term is translated as "I <u>am confident</u>" and in 2 Timothy 1:12 where it is rendered "I <u>am convinced</u>" (with "I" being a separate first-person pronoun in both cases).

So — by all means — be sure to obey what your spiritual leaders **have proven to be true** from God's Word as confirmed in your own study time with the help of your Counselor (1 John 2:27). But never blindly obey anyone, especially if you sense they're putting on big-headed airs to impress or intimidate.

12

Mentor & Protégé Dynamics

This chapter goes hand-and-hand with the previous one. Notice what the Lord taught on the topic of Christian leadership:

> **"they** [Pharisees and teachers of the law] **love to be greeted with respect in the marketplaces and to be called 'Rabbi' by others.**
> [8] **"But you are not to be called 'Rabbi,' for you have one Teacher, and <u>you are all brothers</u>. [9]And do not call anyone on earth 'father,' for you have one Father, and he is in heaven. [10] Nor are you to be called instructors, for you have one Instructor, the Messiah. [11] <u>The greatest among you will be your servant</u>. [12] For <u>those who exalt themselves will be humbled</u>, and those who humble themselves will be exalted."**
>
> **Matthew 23:7-12**

> **Sitting down, Jesus called the Twelve and said, "Anyone who wants to be first must be the very last, and <u>the servant of all</u>."**
>
> **Mark 9:35**

Christ emphasized that believers "are all brothers (and sisters)" and that the person who wants to be first must become last. This doesn't mean that Christian leaders should be pathetic doormats, as noted last chapter, but it certainly conveys **a humble and equalitarian attitude amongst the brethren and sistren which should increase as we advance in the faith** (and, yes, "sistren" is an actual word).

With this in mind, let's consider some insights on spiritual mentors and protégés. Paul and Timothy are a good example of a mentor/mentee relationship in the New Testament. In such relationships should the protégé concede to the perspective of the mentor even in cases where the mentor is *wrong?* What is the basis for spiritual truth in the body of Christ? God's Word, as observed in 2 Timothy 3:16-17 and 1 Corinthians 4:6.

If the mentee clearly discerns that the mentor is in error should the mentee speak up, particularly if the mentor is trying to "prove" his/her point by mere bluster rather than thorough scriptural evidence? Of course the protégé should speak up, keeping in view that there's a right way and a wrong way to disagree with someone who's over you in the Lord or, at least, older than you. Out of respect for the mentor you'll want to leave room for him or her to keep their dignity because, after all, they are the mentor.

However, what if the mentor refuses to receive the correction simply because he or she is the mentor? If this happens it's an indication of the infection of arrogance — a superiority complex — which isn't a good sign. In such occasions you have no choice but to make a stand with the truth and let the chips fall where they may. If the mentor severs ties with you then shame on him or her.

Sometimes the lines between mentor and mentee are blurred for various reasons. Say, for instance, you read a book, article or blog by a certain minister and proceed to learn many things from him or her, which means that this minister automatically becomes your mentor since you are *learning* from him/her (keeping in mind that protégé means "pupil"). Does this make the minister the ultimate authority on every spiritual topic? Does it mean that you can't legitimately disagree with him or her if it's clear he/she is wrong in one area or another? Of course not. Jesus Christ is the "Chief Shepherd" and fivefold ministers are simply *under* shepherds (1 Peter 5:1-4).

Bear in mind that **spiritually mature** mentors won't be threatened by the questions of a mentee. And disagreements won't aggravate them as long as they can be scripturally proven and are respectful. In fact, **true mentors *want* their pupils to exceed them and therefore they *welcome* questions and contentions as the protégé grows.** Mentors who get irate when mentees merely question them or disagree based on the Scriptures show that they're not spiritually mature; meaning they're not STAGE FOUR.

For anyone who would argue that a protégé *couldn't* possibly reach a point where he/she knows more than the mentor in one area or another, this is frankly silly and unrealistic. After all, David proclaimed he had greater insights and understanding than *his* teachers and elders (Psalm 119:99-100). Why do you think God recorded this in the Holy Scriptures, our blueprint for Christianity and spirituality? Because *this will happen* whenever a person has the same heart of David, meaning "a man (or woman) after God's own heart."

It goes without saying that leaders who resort to bluster, intimidation or insults in biblical discussions eliminate themselves as mentors and show that they're not worthy of your respect (unless they humbly repent, of course). They're spiritually immature and infected by arrogance. *Leave them*, as the Lord instructed (Matthew 15:14). We'll look at this further next chapter.

Lastly, there's only one flawless teacher on Earth during the Church Age and that's the Holy Spirit (John 16:7-13 & 1 John 2:27). Men and women of God — no matter how knowledgeable, gifted and spiritually mature — are human beings and therefore imperfect. They're not infallible or perfect in knowledge and therefore don't know it all. Always remember this: **Those who transfer knowledge can also transfer error.**

Furthermore, human mentors have weaknesses and will inevitably let you down. For all of these reasons you'll naturally move away from *dependency* on human mentors as you advance in the Lord. You'll instead lean more and more on the Holy Spirit; and the Holy Spirit is God (Matthew 28:19 & 2 Corinthians 13:14). Believers who are overly dependent upon human mentors are not spiritually mature. They're in STAGE TWO or, at best, STAGE THREE.

Please notice I said *"dependent upon* human mentors," which is different than *receiving from* them. Those in STAGE FOUR are humble and wise enough to always seek out and receive from other people in their area of expertise and wisdom — in fact, they're enthusiastic about it because they're *learners* who are constantly learning.[11] So receiving from other people's area of strength is

---

[11] Keep in mind that 'disciple' literally means "learner" in the original Greek. Even if a believer is a fivefold minister (e.g. an apostle, prophet or pastor) they're *still* a disciple of Christ, a *learner* of Christ. For details see the article *Disciple — What is it? (The answer might surprise you)* at the FOL site.

always good, but this is different than being perpetually dependent on them, which isn't good.

13

Ministerial Pitfalls and Abuses

A topic like this requires explanation so as not to be misunderstood. Quality ministers are of eminent importance in the lives of believers, as already stressed. I could name several outstanding ministers who were strategic to my spiritual upbringing, which isn't to say I necessarily agree with any of them on every jot & tittle. I don't, but that doesn't negate their monumental contribution to my spiritual health.

Furthermore, 1 Thessalonians 5:12-13 says that believers are to "**respect** those who **work hard among you**, who are over you in the Lord… [and to] **Hold them in the highest regard** in love because of their work." We are to respect those who are over us in the Lord, which refers to fivefold ministers, like pastors and teachers (Ephesians 4:11-13). The reason it specifies respecting those who "work hard among you" is because it's impossible to respect lazy ministers.

For instance, I can't respect ministers who are obviously lazy when it comes to the teaching and preaching of God's Word. Think about it, roughly 50% of every church service is devoted to the ministry of the Word, which is necessary for the feeding, inspiration and growth of believers. As such, you would think that ministers would be *prepared* before they teach or preach and that they'd serve with *all their hearts* (Colossians 3:23), but sometimes I observe ministers just winging it, and you can always tell. This is laziness and it's impossible to respect ministers who give lazy sermons, whether at a home-styled fellowship, a mega-church or anywhere in between.

Speaking of winging sermons, this itself is a form of abuse, albeit the passive kind. How so? Because those who teach/preach the Word are obligated to *feed* and *exhort* believers so that they might mature, not fill the air with hollow sermonizing.

Notice that 1 Thessalonians 5:12-13 says believers are to respect ministers who work hard and are "over you in the Lord." These people are over you *in the Lord*. They're over you at the fellowship that you're a part of, but not in matters of style and taste, like clothing, hair styles, food, romantic interests or types of music, movies and recreation. They're over you *spiritually*, not over you in areas of personal taste.

Also, the passage says to hold hard-working ministers in the highest regard "because of their work." Respect them for *their work* — their calling and anointing from God — and not in regards to items of personal taste. If you think a minister has bad taste in women, too bad, it's his choice. If you don't like her choice of vehicle, it's none of your business. If you don't like the way he prefers to dress at assembly, at home or when he's out and about, too bad, mind your own business. Amen.

The Four Pitfalls of Ministers

The four pitfalls of ministers are:

1. Sexual misconduct.
2. Greed.
3. Arrogance.
4. Legalism, which is sterile religiosity.[12]

It's no surprise that the first three correspond to what the Bible says are the three categories of sin: the **lust of the flesh**, the **lust of the eyes** and the **pride of life** (1 John 2:16). Two well-known ministerial scandals in the late 80s correspond to the first two and, arguably, the first three: Jimmy Swaggart and Jim Baker. All believers, of course, have to be wary of these common pitfalls, how much more so those who aspire to be leaders?

Examples of Ministerial Abuse in the New Testament

Paul founded the Corinthian church on his second missionary journey. He stayed in Corinth for at least a year and a half feeding the believers the Word of God before venturing off to other areas (Acts 18:11). Two or three years later Paul heard some disturbing news about the fellowship so he wrote them a few letters of instruction, encouragement and correction. The epistles known as 1 Corinthians and 2 Corinthians are the two surviving letters. Notice Paul's comments in this passage:

---

[12] My book *Legalism Unmasked* goes into more detail or check out the article *Legalism—Understanding its Many Forms* at the FOL site.

> **<u>You gladly put up with fools</u> since you are so wise! [20] In fact, you even put up with anyone <u>who enslaves you</u> or <u>exploits you</u> or <u>takes advantage of you</u> or <u>pushes himself forward</u> or <u>slaps you in the face</u>. [21] To my shame I admit that we were too weak for that!**
>
> **2 Corinthians 11:19-21**

During Paul's absence some arrogant authoritarians rose up and were abusing the believers. He blatantly calls these corrupt leaders "fools." Paul then details five ways in which the authoritarians were abusing the believers:

- **"Enslaves you"**: This refers to a general atmosphere of bondage, including excessive rules that quench the spirit of freedom in Christ (Galatians 5:1 & Colossians 2:20-23).
- **"Exploits you"**: 'Exploit' means "to use selfishly for one's own ends." This likely applies to undue demands for financial support in light of the fact that the same Greek word is used in Luke 20:47 to describe Jesus' denouncement of legalists' "*devouring* widows' houses".
- **"Takes advantage of you"**: This applies to all manner of manipulation, including intimidation and social pressure.
- **"Pushes himself forward"**: This refers to lording it over people with a tyrannical air, something which fivefold ministers *aren't* supposed to do.
- **"Slaps you in the face"**: Apparently the legalists resorted to physical abuse to humiliate the believers, but this could also be a figurative reference to degrading abuse in general. Either way, both are wrong. Abuse is the misuse of power.

Paul then points out in verse 21 that he never resorted to these types of fleshly tactics when he established this church in Corinth.

Why didn't he? Because Paul was a *godly* minister and not one poisoned by arrogance and legalism.

All five of these practices are typical of authoritarians and are condemned in Scripture. Please be aware of each and don't tolerate it if any should surface in your fellowship.

Pastors are NOT Supposed to "Lord it Over" People

While we briefly addressed this topic in chapter **5**, let's look at it in more detail now:

> **To the elders among you, I appeal as a fellow elder, a witness of Christ's sufferings and one who also will share in the glory to be revealed: [2]Be shepherds [pastors] of <u>God's flock</u> that is <u>under your care</u>, <u>serving as overseers</u> — not because you must, but because you are willing, as God wants you to be; not greedy for money, but eager <u>to serve</u>; [3] <u>not lording it over those entrusted to you</u>, but being examples to the flock. [4]And when <u>the Chief Shepherd</u> appears, you will receive the crown of glory that will never fade away.**
>
> **1 Peter 5:1-4**

As you can see in verses 2-3, the New Testament outright denounces the practice of ministers "lording it over" others. The word "lording" here means to control, subjugate or rule in the sense of being the ultimate authority. Although pastors are certainly the authority of the fellowships they oversee, Christ is the ultimate authority of the Church, which is why he's referred to as the "*Chief* Shepherd" in verse 3. **Pastors simply have no business overbearingly controlling believers as if they are the supreme and final authority in their lives.**

Since the passage clearly states that pastors are to serve as "overseers" and not lord it over those entrusted to their care, whatever else 'oversee' means, we can be sure that it does *not* mean to bully people in a domineering manner.

It's important to understand how spiritual leaders are to oversee others so we don't allow them to oversee us in the wrong way. Ministers are to oversee in a *protective* sense and in a *directive* sense:

- They are **protective** in the sense of guarding people from false teachers and their false doctrines, not to mention wolves in general, whether legalists or libertines (which are two sides of the same bad coin).
- They are **directive** in the sense of directing the affairs of the assembly and giving people their Spirit-led vision for the ministry. This includes granting believers the encouragement and opportunity to excel in their gifting and calling within the framework of that vision.

It goes without saying that overseeing others in these senses has nothing to do with lording it over them.

Authoritarianism is demagoguery where the Christian leader tries to dominate others through intimidation and manipulation. But this is an oxymoron since 'minister' literally means "servant" and reveals how Christian ministers are to minister — with a servant's heart. This isn't to say, of course, that ministers have to be perpetually sugary sweet as there's a time and place for Spirit-led rebuke, like when Paul openly corrected Peter for his legalism

(Galatians 2:11-14) or when Jesus boldly cleared the temple of fools (Mark 11:15-18).

There was a large church in my area where the pastor had an overtly authoritarian spirit. I know because I heard many of his sermons on radio and cassette, as well as knew members from the assembly, like my boss (at the time) and his wife. This pastor had an overwhelming air and it was easy to see why people would follow him, but I didn't sense any love or joy in his words.

I developed a friendship with a man who attended this assembly for a few months. Some of his relatives and friends were members, but they were so wowed by the pastor's natural leadership qualities that they failed to see his potentially harmful spirit.

My friend wasn't so wowed. He said he visited the church many times before deciding not to stay. He told his relatives and friends, "He's a charismatic speaker and all, but I don't see any love or joy there." It wasn't much later that there were two mass exoduses over a period of about a year. By this point the assembly had a bad reputation in the community and it never really recovered. The pastor died prematurely a dozen years later.

Before its breakdown and decline there were red flags of authoritarianism everywhere:

- Congregants had to get the pastor's approval for large purchases, like a refrigerator;
- If someone left the fellowship his/her relatives and friends were instructed to cut all ties;
- People were encouraged to quit their well-paying jobs and start their own businesses;

- Men with longer hair were pressured to cut it and maintain shorter hair length;
- The entrance gates were closed and the doors locked during services;
- Believers were discouraged from going to the restroom during the ridiculously long Sunday services;
- Individuals were literally screamed at in front of the congregation if the pastor thought they were going astray; etc.

If you've ever seen the film *Guyana Tragedy: The Story of Jim Jones*, this church was bordering on being that authoritarian.

Since the Bible plainly teaches that pastors are not to "lord it over" believers, they have no business telling congregants where to work, how to wear their hair, what kind of car to buy, what kind of clothes to wear, what style of music to listen to, what kind of movies to watch, etc. They're not the final authority in believers' lives, God is.

The believer should simply be fed the Word of God and encouraged to develop a relationship with the Lord. This includes teaching them important principles of wisdom like how to guard their hearts as the wellspring of life so that negative, evil things don't get planted within (Proverbs 4:23). As they grow they'll naturally make their *own* decisions about these types of things, as led of the Holy Spirit. I'm not saying, by the way, that pastors shouldn't encourage modest apparel; that's a no-brainer.

Authoritarian Tactics: Bluster, Intimidations and Insults

Arrogant authoritarians typically resort to bluster, intimidation and unnecessary insults in confrontations, even casual ones in which you're simply discussing biblical topics. A couple of ministers I met, for instance, had the tendency to "prove" their points through bluster or intimidation rather than what the Bible clearly and consistently teaches.

When you come across these types you have to resist the temptation to stoop to their level. Ignore their covert (and sometimes overt) insults & intimidation and simply focus on the relevant biblical data. When they see that you won't submit to their manipulations they'll either **1.** get more insulting and abusive or **2.** end the discussion one way or another (if it's an email exchange, for example, they'll simply refuse to write back under the assumed guise that they're "too busy").

In cases of the former, continue to resist the temptation to respond in kind and focus on what the Word of God teaches in a balanced fashion, interpreting Scripture with Scripture. Only revert to tough love tactics if led of the Holy Spirit to do so, which Jesus did on occasion (e.g. Luke 11:37-53 & Matthew 23:13-33).

Whatever the case, you must not tolerate or condone this kind of pompous abuse — tactics of bluster and intimidation — even if the minister has an impressive ministry and decades of experience. If the individual is truly a great man or woman of God then he/she has no business behaving in this manner. If it's someone over you in the LORD you're still obligated to correct. Of course, you should correct in a respectful manner, particularly if the person is older than you (1 Peter 5:5), unless the situation calls for a more blunt approach.

I've known big-time ministers who seem to have let it go to their head and are therefore rigid with the box into which they've put God (and themselves). If you happen to share a legitimate scriptural point that deviates from a dubious doctrine they've taught as gospel truth for decades they'll get irate and rashly insult you.

Spiritually mature believers, by contrast, don't get mad when someone merely disagrees with them; they humbly and honestly turn to God's Word and allow it to settle the matter in a thorough and balanced manner. In short, mature believers allow the word of truth (John 17:17 & 2 Timothy 2:15) to reveal what's true and what's not true or, in some cases, what's partially true. This will correct the other person. If he or she still disagrees then that's their problem.

I've noticed, unfortunately, that too many believers — including fivefold ministers — don't go by the authority of God's Word, but rather by the 'authority' of religious tradition and the forefathers or foremothers of their camp, whatever/whoever those might be.

For instance, if you say something thoroughly biblical that disagrees with a religious slogan of their sect or what the founder teaches they'll immediately put up a wall and the case will be closed. Why? Because they respect the word of a human authority above the Word of God. People like this, no matter how great their position, are still locked into the childhood stage of Christianity (1 John 2:12-14) — STAGE TWO — even though they may have a foot or hand in the next two stages. It's frankly a puerile mindset.

Thankfully, I've known world-traveling ministers with impressive ministries who are quite humble. For instance, I've met some great ministers face-to-face to discuss scriptural topics and their humility was palpable. I've met with other ministers whose ministries are 1/50th the size of these, but who were noticeably arrogant about their supposedly great position and accomplishments, the latter of which weren't very impressive.

It's impossible for these types to relate to fellow believers as equals and they therefore tend to speak down to them or intimidate, even if it's subtle. I find it amusing whenever I see it, but not in a good way. They tend to posture and bloviate like they're great men or women of God when it's simply not the case. How do I know? Because God actively opposes the proud but gives favor to the humble. See for yourself:

> **"God opposes the proud but shows favor to the humble."**   **James 4:6 & 1 Peter 5:5**

The passage is in quotes because James and Peter are paraphrasing Proverbs 3:34. Consequently, the verse appears no less than *three times in God's Word* — once in the Old Testament and twice in the New Testament. Do ya think the LORD is trying to tell us something? Obviously: God *resists* the arrogant — *opposes* them — but extends favor and honor to the humble.

If the Lord resists and opposes the proud, including those who say they're Christians and even function in the ministry, then he's obviously not close to them, right? And if God's not close to the person they're obviously not spiritually mature because believers who are spiritually mature know and walk humbly before God.

Notice what this psalm says about the humble and the arrogant, along with how our Creator regards both:

> **Though the LORD is highly exalted,**
>> **yet he pays attention to those who are lowly regarded** [the humble],
>> **but he is aware of the arrogant** [only] **from afar.**
>
> **Psalm 138:6** (ISV)

Arrogant ministers — no matter how long they've been in the ministry and how great their accomplishments — are *not* close to God, regardless of their claims otherwise. **It is impossible for the LORD to be close to an arrogant person!** God only knows such people from a distance.

Needless to say, spiritual mentors who resort to bluster, intimidation or invalid insults in discussions disqualify themselves as mentors; they're not worthy of your respect. *FLEE* from unworthy "mentors" who utilize such carnal measures or who show signs of envy & rivalry without repentance. If you don't, you can be sure you'll regret it one day.

The Spirit of Condemnation

A spirit of condemnation is when a minister regularly tears down and 'beats up' a congregation, which is an abuse of the pulpit. Such ministers tend to motivate others based on shame. For example, they'll say things like: "You're not reading the Word of God like you should! And you call yourself a Christian?" The root of this type of wicked spirit is arrogance, which is a superiority complex.

When these types of ministers tear down others they automatically elevate themselves. Its fleshly pride and it's truly sad when ministers fall into such a religionist rut. Sometimes they never get out and, if they do, it's likely due to intense intercession or because someone dared to walk in tough love with them.

The spirit of condo is at odds with the true ministerial spirit, which Paul summed up when he spoke of the authority ministers have for **building believers up** and *not* tearing them down (2 Corinthians 10:8 & 13:10). He also stressed this in our main text where he detailed the purpose of all fivefold ministers: "to prepare God's people for works of service, so that the body of Christ may be **built up**" (Ephesians 4:11-13).

You don't have to be a spiritual Einstein to recognize a spirit of condemnation. Years ago my sister, Jennifer, was looking for a church in Southern California and ended up visiting one for a few Sundays, but she decided not to stay. Why? Because after all three services she left feeling **beat up and condemned** rather than inspired and encouraged. Needless to say, only a glutton for punishment would stay in such an assembly.

This isn't to suggest, of course, that there's no place for denouncing sins and encouraging repentance in church services. Skilled ministers who are led of the Spirit will bring about a spirit of repentance through the ministry of the Word, but will also remove the burden of guilt, instill the Lord's peace and motivate individuals onward. In other words, even though they denounce sin and spur repentance their ministry is encouraging and inspiring. This is the minister's job.

A good example of this can be seen in Yeshua after his resurrection. He appeared to two of the disciples who were understandably discouraged because of his unjust crucifixion. The risen Christ met up with them as they were walking along the road and they talked for a bit, but they were somehow prevented from recognizing him. After Jesus departed, the two disciples reflected on the encounter: "Were not our hearts burning within us while he talked with us on the road and opened the Scriptures to us?" (Luke 24:32).

This is the effect Christ-like ministers should have on believers. You know you're at a healthy church when you leave a service with your heart burning with inspiration and you see things in God's Word you never saw before.

Luke 24 goes on to show us what the Lord did weeks later when he ascended: "he lifted up his hands and **blessed them**. While he was **blessing them**, he left them and was taken up into heaven" (verses 50-51). Even as the Messiah was leaving this Earth to go to the Father he was **blessing people** — it was the last thing he did before going to the Father! **This is how Christ-like ministers should be — constantly blessing people and building them up,** *not* **condemning them and tearing down.**

Since the spirit of condemnation is rooted in arrogance (tearing others down to build oneself up); it's also a spirit of authoritarianism. This is when a "minister" leads by trying to bully people, which is plainly condemned in Scripture, as noted in the afore-cited key passage, 1 Peter 5:1-4.

Verses 1-2 of that passage show that Paul was specifically addressing "elders," mature believers, who were called to serve as "shepherds," that is, pastors or overseers. He goes on to say that they should be eager to "serve," meaning minister. This is important because pastors who regularly tear down their subordinates are essentially grumps who have lost the joyful eagerness of serving as shepherds of God's flock. In such cases, pastoring has become more of a job than a joy. This can always be seen on their faces; instead of the joy of serving there's the scowl of forced labor.

14

The Diotrephes Spirit vs. the Davidic Spirit

I see too much rivalry in the Church today, even in leadership. This is nothing new, of course, as Paul had to deal with it in the early Church, 2000 years ago (Philippians 1:15). Unfortunately, there are some ministers who view anyone who's knowledgeable and gifted with an eye of evil suspicion. They don't want anyone "stealing their thunder," so they turn people against those they deem rivals, sometimes even resorting to slander, as unbelievable as that may seem. In fact, they'll cite the gifts of the Spirit to back up their smear campaigns, e.g. "I discerned by the Spirit that he (or she) is here to provoke disunity and to do the devil's work."

Of course there *are* people who cause serious problems and they need to be corrected and possibly even driven out when necessary, but such people are proud mockers and will show clear signs of the flesh (Proverbs 22:10, Romans 16:17-18 & Titus 3:9-11). That's not who I'm referring to here. I'm talking about solid, fruit-bearing Christians who are slandered and chased out of assemblies because pastors or elders feel threatened by them. Such rivalry is rooted in jealousy, insecurity and selfish ambition (Philippians 1:15-17). They're **weak "leaders,"** pure and simple.

As briefly noted in chapter **10**, there's a good example of this in the Bible:

> **I wrote to the church, but Diotrephes, <u>who loves to be first, will not welcome us.</u> [10] So when I come, I will call attention to what he is doing, <u>spreading malicious nonsense about us.</u> Not satisfied with that, <u>he even refuses to welcome other believers.</u> He also stops those who want to do so and <u>puts them out of the church.</u>**
>
> **3 John 3:9-10**

Here the apostle John cites a leader of one of the churches he oversaw — Diotrephes (*dye-OT-rah-feez*) — who refused to welcome John and other godly ministers to minister at the assembly. This guy even ran a smear campaign against them (!). Those in the congregation who objected to Diotrephes' carnal tactics were booted out by the man!

This reveals that Diotrephes was the pastor of the fellowship since only a pastor would have the authority to prevent an overseer of John's stature from coming and ministering, not to mention it's the pastor who has the final word on who is excommunicated from the assembly.

So why do some commentators act like it's unclear that Diotrephes was the pastor? Perhaps because this is a frank biblical account of a corrupted fivefold minister and these commentators (who are ministers themselves) are understandably hesitant to mar the image of pastors to the public. Yet this account doesn't mar the image of pastors, it just conveys the unfortunate truth that real-life ministers can become corrupted by giving-in to the flesh, as detailed last chapter.

Speaking of which, John readily understood Diotrephes' root problem — he loved to be first (verse 9). In other words, Diotrephes was a pompous control-freak who wasn't interested in serving others, but rather wanted others to serve him. Such a mindset is, of course, in direct opposition to Christ & Paul's attitude of servant-leadership, not to mention Peter (Matthew 23:1-11, 2 Corinthians 10:8, 13:10 & 1 Peter 5:2-3).

John may have been renowned for his loving spirit, but he wasn't about to overlook such heinous abuses in the name of peace and niceness; no, he was fully intent on exposing and correcting the man (verse 10). In fact, John's third epistle was/is **a public judgment and exposal of Diotrephes' error to every person who has read it ever since**. This includes *you,* right now. It's a form of tough love.

Sad to say, there are ungodly "ministers" in the Church today just like Diotrephes. Mature Christians need to boldly rise up and call attention to the abuses of these selfish control-freaks whenever such abuse occur, like John did, even at the threat of excommunication or losing one's ministry gig. After all, evil thrives when good people do nothing! (Speaking of which, there's nothing more pathetic than weak 'yes men' or 'yes women' who condone corruption in the name of meekness or due to idolization of a relationship or position).

Strong leaders, by contrast, are able to utilize strong people and properly integrate them in their work. Take the example of David, "a man after God's own heart"…

David Wasn't Threatened by His "Mighty Men"

The Bible goes into quite a bit of detail about David's "mighty men," which were some 53 individuals who helped David become king of Israel (2 Samuel 23:8-39 & 1 Chronicles 11:10-47). They formed David's inner circle of leadership. These powerful men were *more skilled than David* in their areas of expertise (!). Yet David knew his calling and strengths, and was therefore secure and unthreatened. He also knew his limitations. He realized that he wasn't going to make it alone because no one makes it alone — *no one*. All great men and women embrace the help and skills of others.

Consequently, David enlisted this formidable group to assist him in fulfilling God's assignment. In short, David didn't automatically view gifted people with an eye of evil suspicion and chase them away. No, he wisely recognized their uniqueness & greatness and released them to operate in their strengths on his team. Thus David became the greatest king of Israel. Oh, that there were more leaders like David in the Church today!

Needless to say, **Go where you are celebrated and encouraged to walk in your strengths and not where you're tolerated, ignored, suppressed or slandered**.

<u>15</u>

When Ministers Fail to Correct Their Relatives in the Church

Have you ever experienced a situation at an assembly where the pastor refuses to genuinely correct a carnal individual because they're related? For instance, Carol & I were part of a ministry years ago where a pathological liar ran around the church gossiping & slandering, yet was tolerated because she was related to the pastor and very much favored. It goes without saying that this caused constant problems in that fellowship.

The "Eli Syndrome"

I call this the "Eli Syndrome" based on the biblical account of Eli, the priest of Shiloh, and his tolerance of his wicked sons, who served at the Tabernacle or, more accurately, served *themselves*. Accounts like this are chronicled in the Old Testament as warnings to us so that we don't commit the same folly (Romans 15:4 & 1 Corinthians 10:11). Let's read the account:

<u>Eli's sons were scoundrels; they had no regard for the LORD</u>. ¹³Now it was the practice of the priests that, whenever any of the people offered a sacrifice, the priest's servant would come with a three-pronged fork in his hand while the meat was being boiled ¹⁴and would plunge the fork into the pan or kettle or caldron or pot. Whatever the fork brought up the priest would take for himself. This is how they treated all the Israelites who came to Shiloh. ¹⁵But even before the fat was burned, the priest's servant would come and say to the person who was sacrificing, "Give the priest some meat to roast; he won't accept boiled meat from you, but only raw."

¹⁶If the person said to him, "Let the fat be burned first, and then take whatever you want," the servant would answer, "No, hand it over now; if you don't, I'll take it by force."

¹⁷<u>This sin of the young men was very great in the LORD's sight, for they were treating the LORD's offering with contempt</u>...

²²Now <u>Eli, who was very old, heard about everything his sons were doing to all Israel and how they slept with the women who served at the entrance to the tent of meeting</u>. ²³So he said to them, "Why do you do such things? I hear from all the people about <u>these wicked deeds of yours</u>. ²⁴No, my sons; the report I hear spreading among the LORD's people is not good. ²⁵If one person sins against another, God may mediate for the offender; but if anyone sins against the LORD, who will intercede for them?" His sons, however, did not listen to their father's rebuke,

for it was the LORD's will to put them to death.[13]

1 Samuel 2:12-17, 22-25

Eli's two sons were "in the ministry" but are described as wicked scoundrels who had no regard for the LORD and even fornicated with the young women who served at the Tabernacle (verses 12, 17 & 22)! Although Eli rebuked his beloved offspring at one point it's clear that his heart wasn't in it and the sons continued in their wicked ways without consequence (verses 22-25).

How do we explain this? Eli loved his sons, as any parent, but he foolishly only loved them with soft, gentle love. This was a huge mistake and ultimately resulted in God's judgment, which entailed the premature death of both sons, as well as the capture of the Ark of the Covenant, Eli's own death, the death of his daughter-in-law and the departure of God's anointing from Eli's direct bloodline. These things are chronicled in 1 Samuel 4:11 and 4:18-22.

As far as the departure of God's anointing goes, Eli's orphaned grandson was given the name Ichabod, which means "no glory" or "the glory has departed" (1 Samuel 4:21). This shows that **God's glory will depart from any ministry that allows the Eli Syndrome!** Needless to say, if you are a minister and don't want God's anointing to leave your ministry, do *not* permit the Eli Syndrome.

This tragedy could have been avoided if only Eli was willing to love his sons with the necessary tough love, which would involve more than just a half-hearted verbal correction. It would mean a

---

[13] Don't stumble over the peculiar phrasing of the second part of verse 25. The punishment of Eli's sons was due to their *own* rebellion. Writers in the Old Testament simply categorized events as falling under the LORD's sovereign control, even disobedience.

stern public rebuke and removal from the ministry altogether until they humbly repented and proved themselves. Loving his sons solely with gentle love resulted in their deaths whereas implementing tough love would have saved them.

In other words, tough love would have literally saved their lives, not to mention Eli's ministry. It goes without saying that tough love is sometimes necessary. It's a good thing, not bad.

Interestingly, Eli's protégé, Samuel, also fell prey to the "Eli Syndrome": He foolishly appointed his two ungodly sons as judges in Israel in his old age (1 Samuel 8:1-5). Why didn't he seek out two *godly* people to serve as Israel's leaders? Because the Eli Syndrome causes otherwise God-fearing ministers to unwisely turn a blind eye to the glaring sins of their kin.

You'll sometimes see evidence of this Eli Syndrome in today's churches or ministries. A minister will grant status to some undeserving kin, usually children, grandchildren or siblings, which doesn't necessarily have to be an official position. The minister will then tend to condone the relatives' carnal actions, making excuses for them, etc. As long as other believers get along with these relatives they'll have the minister's favor, but if they dare take a stand against any fleshliness they'll be blacklisted one way or another and eventually compelled to leave.

Like Eli, the minister may offer a weak verbal correction for appearances' sake while the relatives continue to wreak havoc, overtly or covertly. There's only one sad end to the Eli Syndrome: The corruption of the ministry as sin works like yeast through the dough of the fellowship and the inevitable departure of God's presence and anointing (1 Corinthians 5:6-8). If only the minister would implement tough love!

What Was Wrong with Taking RAW Meat Rather than BOILED Meat?

For those interested, I wanted to include an explanation of the curious transgression of Eli's sons chronicled in 1 Samuel 2:12-15. Eli's sons, Hophni and Phinehas, were subordinate priests at the Tabernacle in Shiloh and they committed three violations of the Law in this situation:

1. They took what was not theirs. The priests were due the breast and a thigh of each fellowship offering, as observed in Leviticus 7:34 and 10:14-15, but Eli's sons took for themselves whatever a huge 3-pronged fork would collect from the boiling pot.
2. They took for themselves before they gave the LORD his portion — that is, before the fat was burned on the altar (Leviticus 7:25 & 7:31).
3. They demanded raw meat so that they could roast it slowly rather than boiling it quickly as the sacrificial law prescribed. By doing so, they mocked the LORD's instructions at the first Passover to cook and eat food quickly before escaping Egypt (Exodus 12:11).

As such, Eli's sons were not only depriving God's people of their portions of the peace offerings; worse, they were depriving the LORD.

16

New Covenant Prophets and Judging Prophecies

It is necessary to address New Testament prophets in more detail than in chapter **3** because of misunderstandings about this gift. Let's do a quick recap and jump into additional material.

I've heard it erroneously taught that when a prophet prophesies over a believer the individual is obligated to obey the prophecy to the letter and church leaders are to hold him/her accountable to it.

Here are a couple examples: If a believer feels she wants to leave the assembly — for whatever reason — but is informed she must stay because it was prophesied that she *belonged* to that church. Or if the believer intends on going to college or start a career but he's told he can't because the prophet prophesied that he was to be a missionary to Africa. Absurd, you say? It's been known to happen, typically in Pentecostal fellowships that adopt an authoritarian spirit.

This is a case of using the gift of prophecy to manipulate people, which is condemned in the New Testament. It's a form of bondage, not to mention authoritarian abuse, where the prophet's words are viewed as the spoken Word of God in which the believer cannot disagree.

While the word of prophecy is a wonderful gift from the LORD and important in the Church this does not condone the abuse of it wherein people are made to feel like they're in bondage to a prophetic word that may, in fact, be off or even completely wrong. Nor does it condone the dictatorial antics of prophets who think their prophecies are the Word of God which must be blindly accepted and obeyed to the letter.

The reason such abuse exists is because believers are largely ignorant of the gift of prophecy in the New Testament era. They confuse the office of the Old Testament prophet with that of the New Testament prophet. This shouldn't be done because they are very different.

In the Old Testament, what the prophet said was equal to the Word of the LORD and kings made extremely important decisions at their word, like going to war. The primary purpose of the Old Testament prophet was to lead and guide Israel via the Word of the LORD and, in fact, a lot of their words became Holy Scripture, which we know today as the prophetic books of the Old Testament.

For this reason, the words of a prophet had to be 100% accurate. If their words were proven to be false they were to no longer be regarded as prophets and were even to be put to death (Deuteronomy 18:20-22). If an Old Testament prophet missed it *just once*, they were done. This, of course, didn't happen in cases where the king and other leaders were corrupt and actually *wanted* false prophets to comfort them with lies, which occurred all too often in Israel and Judah. (Chapter **10** features an example or two).

Jesus Christ has replaced the Old Testament prophet in the New Testament (Hebrews 1:1-2). He's *The* **Prophet** that the Hebrews had been expecting for almost 1500 years (Deuteronomy 18:15, John 6:14 & 7:40).

The New Covenant prophet is different from the Old Covenant prophet. The gift of prophecy was not given to the body of Christ for the purpose of leading and guiding God's people because believers are born-again spiritually and have the Holy Spirit *within them* for this very purpose. As Jesus said: "But when he, the Spirit of truth, comes, he will guide you into all truth. He will not speak on his own; he will speak only what he hears, and he will tell you what is yet to come" (John16:13).

Since it is the Holy Spirit's job to guide believers in the New Testament era, we don't need the gift of prophecy for this function, as was the case in the Old Testament. So if a prophet prophesies over you and says you're to do this or that and go here or there, don't receive it unless the Spirit has *already* been leading you in that direction.

In other words, prophecies in the New Testament are to *confirm* what the Holy Spirit has *already* been leading you to do. You could say it's an external source to confirm or compliment the believer's internal source of direction from God. I suppose it's possible that the order could be reversed, particularly in cases where the believer isn't sensitive to the moving of the Spirit, but both external and internal should match up.

How do you know if the Holy Spirit is leading you to do something or not do something? The Bible says you are to "let the peace of Christ rule in your heart" (Colossians 3:15). In the Greek "rule" means govern. Say if you have a decision to make and you've prayed about it, as shown in Proverbs 3:6. How do you know what God wants you to do? Simple: What do you have a peace about doing? Which course of action do you have a 'good feeling' about? That's the direction you should take. You'll naturally become better at this as you grow in the Lord.

There may be times, of course, when this is somewhat inapplicable because the prophet may warn you of a *forthcoming* situation, like a job loss or some kind of disaster. The purpose of this type of prophecy is to prepare you and encourage you to get through the negative situation.

This was the function of Agabus' prophecy to Paul when he warned him of the severe persecutions he was going to face in Jerusalem, which we'll look at momentarily. With these types of prophecies, if the event doesn't come to pass then the prophet obviously missed it and I'd be a little leery the next time he or she gives such a word.

In the New Testament era you are *not* in bondage to the words of some prophet who likes to throw his/her weight around. You are to be led and guided by the Holy Spirit, not a prophet. So if some prophet prophesies over you and it doesn't bear witness with your spirit, throw it out! Never allow yourself to be manipulated into doing something you don't have a peace from God about doing.

Judging Prophecies

I want to prove to you beyond any shadow of doubt that you are not obligated to accept any prophecy that you don't have a peace about in your spirit. In fact, the New Testament *repeatedly* instructs believers to *judge prophecies* before embracing them.

Let's look at three such passages, starting with this one:

Dear friends, do not believe every spirit, but <u>test the spirits</u> to see whether they are from God, because many <u>false prophets</u> have gone out into the world.

1 John 4:1

The issue is false prophets and their false prophesies, which is why John encourages believers to "test the spirits," meaning to try or examine the prophecy in question. If you have to test the prophecy then there's a possibility that it might be wrong.

How do you test prophecies? **1.** By the Word of God and **2.** by the leading of the Holy Spirit in your spirit (Ephesians 3:16). If a prophet says to a married woman, "You are to attend to my sexual needs" it can be thrown out as a false prophecy because it violates the morality of the Bible; in fact, the "prophet" himself should no longer be considered a prophet since his "fruit" has exposed him as false (Matthew 7:15-23). If a prophet tells you to quit your job in order to do such-and-such for the church and you don't have a peace about it then don't accept it.

My wife, Carol, was at an assembly where a pastor exhorted her to do secretarial work for the church, even though they already had a secretary who didn't work outside the church. This was to free-up the current secretary to concentrate more on leading in worship or what have you. Carol rejected this "word from the Lord" right away because she already had her hands full with a full-time job as a general manager. More importantly, she didn't discern any moving of the Spirit to do secretarial work in her spare time. None. She didn't have a peace about it (Colossians 3:15).

The pastor who gave this word may have been a sincere man of God, but he missed it on this occasion because the Spirit wasn't speaking to the other person (in this case, Carol). The Holy Spirit never brings confusion and conflict to members of the body of Christ, but rather comfort and peace (although the Spirit will convict of sin, of course).

Let's look at another passage:

> **Be joyful always;** [17] **pray continually;** [18] **give thanks in all circumstances, for this is God's will for <u>you</u> in Christ Jesus.**
> [19] **Do not put out the Spirit's fire;** [20] <u>**do not treat prophecies with contempt.**</u> [21] <u>**Test everything.**</u> <u>**Hold on to the good.**</u>
>
> **1 Thessalonians 5:16-21**

The reason I include verses 16-18 in this quote is to show that Paul was addressing *all believers* in Thessalonica and, as such, his words apply to *all believers* today.

With that understanding, he says that we are not to treat prophecies with contempt, meaning we should never look down on the gift of prophecy. Why would a believer be tempted to look down on prophesying? Because those who prophesy are not always 100% correct. You heard that right. They're not always completely accurate. Let me explain.

New Testament prophets speak by unction, that is, by spiritual influence. They pick something up in the spirit and speak by faith from there. Everything in our covenant is by faith. Since those with the gift of prophecy are human beings and human beings are imperfect, it's always possible for a person who's prophesying to be inaccurate in some ways, even though they're legitimately picking something up in the spirit. It might simply be a matter of immaturity or inexperience where they have not yet fully learned to distinguish the vile (flesh) from the precious (spirit).

For instance, some with the gift of prophecy may legitimately pick something up in the spirit but wrap their prophecy in their pet doctrine or conviction. They might say, for instance, "Yay, I the LORD love thee and you are greatly blessed; now go out and witness door-to-door in your neighborhood." In this case the prophet had an encouraging word from the Lord, but then throws in his *own* conviction.

This explains why Paul added "Test everything. Hold on to the good" *after* instructing believers not to regard prophecies with contempt. Why? Because it's possible for the prophecy to be partially right-on and partially off. Keep in mind that there were no verse numbers in the original text; verses 20 and 21 go together. In verse 20 Paul's talking about prophecies and then instructs the believers in verse 21 to test or judge every prophecy with the conclusion that they are to hold on to the good, meaning that which applies or is accurate.

Say a prophet gives you a personal prophecy but only two-thirds of it bears witness with your spirit. The rest of it doesn't apply, and you know it. Should you discard the entire prophecy? No. Paul says to hold on to what is good. The rest of it should be thrown out or, at most, put on the shelf until you have a peace about it.

Are you getting what God's Word is saying? Don't despise prophecies just because people with this gift miss it in certain ways now and then. The prophetic word is good because it encourages believers to move forward and fulfill their calling, as detailed in chapter **3**. But don't blindly embrace every jot and tittle prophesied over you; only accept what you have a peace about, as confirmed by the Holy Spirit. Put the rest aside or throw it out entirely, if necessary. But please don't throw out the person who prophesies — or their ministry — unless of course their "fruit" has exposed them as false (Matthew 7:15-23).

Let's look at one final passage on this matter:

> **Two or three <u>prophets</u> should speak, <u>and the others should weigh carefully what is said</u>. [30]And if a revelation comes to someone who is sitting down, the first speaker should stop. [31] For you can all prophesy in turn so that everyone may be instructed and encouraged. [32] The spirits of prophets are subject to the control of prophets. [33]For God is not a God of disorder but of peace**
>
> **1 Corinthians 14:29-33**

This passage specifically addresses the New Testament prophet. It's not talking about someone in the body who gives a prophecy (Romans 12:6-8), but rather those who are in the office of a prophet, which is part of the fivefold ministry (Ephesians 4:11-13). Like the two other passages above, this one stresses that believers should weigh carefully what the prophet says, meaning examine and judge it.

Some have suggested that "the others" refers to other prophets, as if the only valid people who can test the prophecy of a prophet are other prophets. This is not true for four reasons:

1. The two previous passages we looked at say that *believers in general* are to examine and judge prophetic words. Why would this passage change that? Scripture interprets Scripture.

2. The natural reading of the text shows that "the others" refers to the same people Paul was addressing in verse 26 where he said, "What then shall we say, *brothers and sisters*? When you come together, *each of you* has a hymn, or a word of instruction, a revelation, a tongue or an interpretation."

3. Since Paul was clearly addressing all believers in verse 26 he would have naturally specified who "the others" were in verse 29 *if* he was referring specifically to prophets, but he didn't.

4. The notion that only another fivefold prophet can judge a prophet's words simply doesn't make sense and creates obvious difficulties. What if there's no other prophet present at the church gathering, which is often the case? Would the believers have to blindly embrace what the prophet says, including the pastor? Even if there are other prophets present, wouldn't it be silly for the pastor to have to turn to another prophet and ask, "Is what he said true?" What if two or three prophets got into cahoots and agreed to agree with one another's prophecy? In short, the notion that only another prophet can judge a prophet's prophecy opens the door to authoritarian abuse.

In summary, it's the believer's responsibility to examine and judge prophecies based on God's Word and the leading of the Holy Spirit within, hold on to what is applicable and throw out what isn't. This is a good thing — a wise thing — because it protects the believer from abuse, including manipulation to do things that aren't God's will for their lives.

The Example of Agabus the Prophet

All of this information is wonderful, but it helps to see an actual example from the Scriptures, so let's look at Agabus. He was a New Testament prophet; a good and respected prophet. Notice how he successfully predicted a famine:

> **During this time <u>some prophets</u> came down from Jerusalem to Antioch. [28] <u>One of them, named Agabus</u>, stood up and <u>through the Spirit predicted that a severe famine would spread over the entire Roman world. (This happened during the reign of Claudius.)</u> [29] The disciples, each according to his ability, <u>decided to provide help</u> for the brothers living in Judea. [30] This they did, sending their gift to the elders by Barnabas and Saul.**
>
> **Acts 11:27-30**

As you can see, Agabus was a prophet. He came to Antioch from Jerusalem with some other prophets and prophesied a famine that would negatively affect the people of Judea. The great historian, Josephus, documented this famine as occurring around 46 AD when Claudius was the Roman emperor. So Agabus was right about the famine and it was good that the Christians at Antioch believed his prophecy and compassionately sent an offering to Judea.

Agabus was obviously a highly respected prophet otherwise the believers wouldn't have sent aid to Judea. Think about it: If some Joe Blow off the street wandered into your fellowship and said there was going to be a famine in a bordering nation would you blindly accept it and dish out the cash? Not likely, and wisely so. This indicates that Agabus was a renowned and respected prophet.

Also notice that the believers "decided to provide help" (verse 29), meaning no one commanded them to give with a dictatorial air. Moreover, this suggests that they *decided* after weighing the prophecy and discerning the leading of the Holy Spirit. They had a peace about it so they generously gave. We should do likewise if someone prophesies something along these lines in our circles, but if you have a bad gut feeling about it I wouldn't go along with it.

I mention this passage to show that Agabus was a good prophet, a respected prophet, and an accurate prophet. However, this doesn't mean he was perfect. If he and other New Testament prophets were 100% right 100% of the time the Scriptures would *not* instruct us to examine and judge their prophecies and hold on to the good. As a matter of fact, Paul had to do just this with another one of Agabus' prophecies:

> **Leaving the next day, we reached Caesarea and stayed at the house of Philip the evangelist, one of the seven. [9] He had four unmarried daughters who prophesied.**
> **[10] After we had been there a number of days, <u>a prophet named Agabus</u> came down from Judea. [11]Coming over to us, <u>he took Paul's belt, tied his own hands and feet with it and said, "The Holy Spirit says, 'In this way the Jews of Jerusalem will bind the owner of this belt and will hand him over to the Gentiles.' "</u>**
>
> **Acts 21:8-11**

Agabus obviously picked up something in the spirit about Paul and proceeded to speak in faith. Notice the impact this prophecy had:

> **When we heard this, we and the people there <u>pleaded with Paul not to go up to Jerusalem.</u> [13]Then Paul answered, "Why are you weeping and breaking my heart? I am ready not only to be bound, but also to die in Jerusalem for the name of the Lord Jesus." [14] When he would not**

> **be dissuaded, we gave up and said, "The Lord's will be done."**
>
> **Acts 21:12-14**

The other believers unwisely accepted Agabus' prophecy at face value and took it in a negative sense, that is, they assumed that it *wasn't* God's will for Paul to go to Jerusalem. They consequently tried to discourage the apostle from going, even to the extent of weeping!

Yet notice that Agabus never said it *wasn't* God's will for Paul to go to Jerusalem, he merely informed him of the intense persecutions he would experience by going there. Acts 23:11 verifies beyond any shadow of doubt that it *was* God's will for the apostle to witness in Jerusalem. With this understanding, the obvious purpose of Agabus' prophecy was to warn Paul of the troubles he was going to face so that he'd have the grace to trust the LORD and persevere when it happened.

After hearing the prophecy and being discouraged by the others who took Agabus' prophecy the wrong way, Paul practiced precisely what he taught: He weighed Agabus' prophecy carefully, held on to the good, and made the decision to go to Jerusalem based on the leading of the Holy Spirit. In other words, Paul had a peace about going to Jerusalem despite Agabus' warning and despite the discouraging antics of fellow believers.

Yet there's more: Agabus' prophecy was good in that it prepared Paul for the severe persecutions he would face in Jerusalem, but the details of his prophecy weren't wholly accurate. Agabus said that the Jews in Jerusalem would bind up Paul's hands and feet and deliver him to the Roman government, but this isn't what happened.

Nine days after arriving in Jerusalem the Jews apprehended Paul for the purpose of murdering him, not to turn him over to the Romans; furthermore, the Romans actually saved Paul from the Jews. The soldiers then bound him with chains and took him into custody, but as soon as they found out Paul was a Roman citizen they released him. This is all detailed in Acts 21:30-33 and 22:25-30.

As you can see, Agabus was a respected prophet and rightly so. He accurately predicted that Paul was going to suffer great persecution in Jerusalem and he was right that the apostle was going to be bound hand and foot. This warning helped prepare Paul for his mission and gave him the grace to persevere when persecuted, but — clearly — some of the details of Agabus' prophecy were off.

What this indicates is that Agabus legitimately picked up something from the Spirit, something Paul needed to hear, but as Agabus spoke in faith he missed some of the details. Frankly, these details are insignificant in the grand scheme of things because it was enough that Paul was warned of the troubles he was about to face. And, remember, Agabus never told Paul not to go to Jerusalem; it was the other believers who mistook his words and tried to stop him from going.

This information is important because it proves that New Testament prophets can miss it even while they legitimately pick something up via their gift. This is why believers must test prophecies by the Word of God and the leading of the Holy Spirit. This is what Paul did and he was blessed because of it.

17

What is a DEACON?

Let's now look at those in the Church who are called to *assist* fivefold ministers in fulfilling their vision.

The Greek word for 'deacon' is *diakonos (dee-AK-on-os),* which literally refers to anyone who performs a service. The deacon is a position in the body of Christ that denotes those who perform service-oriented tasks at fellowships subordinate to the fivefold ministers in servant-leadership. Some examples include ushers, greeters, secretaries, custodians, sound operators, gofers and guards.

These kinds of services are "helps ministry" and vary depending on the unique demands of the particular ministry, culture, time period and needs of the people therein. For instance, sound operators are a fairly new position in the scope of Church history.

Notice what the apostle Paul instructed his protégé Timothy on the deacon position:

> **In the same way, <u>deacons</u> are to be worthy of respect, sincere, not indulging in much wine, and not pursuing dishonest gain. [9]They must keep hold of the deep truths of the faith with a clear conscience. [10]<u>They must first be tested</u>; and then if there is nothing against them, let them serve <u>as deacons</u>…**
>
> **[12] A <u>deacon</u> must be faithful to his wife and must manage his children and his household well. [13]Those who have served well gain an excellent standing and great assurance in their faith in Christ Jesus.**
>
> 1 Timothy 3:8-10,12-13

Not just anyone who *says* they're a Christian can be a deacon. They must first be evaluated by servant-leaders in the ministry and proven to be respectable, honest, not drunkards (or druggies), not lovers-of-money, faithful to his/her spouse and able to effectively manage his/her household. These general qualifications would apply to *anyone* functioning in a service-oriented position at an assembly. After all, would you want the sound operator or camera person at your fellowship to leave the service and commit adultery or fraud in their time off? Obviously not. It would be a bad witness.

How do you distinguish an official deacon from a believer at the fellowship who's simply serving in some manner, like providing coffee or distributing food? You could say that the latter person, while not an official deacon, is a deacon in spirit; and will likely become a deacon before too long.

Paul's instructions on deacons in the context of 1 Timothy (above) refer specifically to the church in Ephesus that Timothy was pastoring, which was located in what is today western Turkey.

While this cultural context called for deacons to be male in that particular region & time period, it does not exclude the possibility of female deacons in every assembly throughout the Church Age since Phoebe was a deacon at the church in Cenchrea (Romans 16:1); and Euodia & Syntyche were deacons as well (Philippians 4:2-3).

As such, Paul's instructions in 1 Timothy 3 cannot be interpreted to mean that *all* deacons must be male during the Church Age. Remember, "there is no male and female, for you are all one in Christ Jesus" (Galatians 3:28 ESV).

If you're a fivefold minister and live in a part of the world where it's best to only have males in deacon positions, like Timothy's situation in Ephesus, then — by all means — do so as led of the Spirit, otherwise having female deacons isn't an issue. The most important thing is that the person in the position be qualified for it, whether male or female. This is why the LORD chose Deborah to lead Israel for 40 years spiritually, politically, legally and militarily (Judges 4-5).

Speaking of the gender of deacons, I've been to myriad assemblies over the last several decades since turning to the Lord in early 1984, and I've noticed that certain deacon positions tend to involve males and others females, with some featuring both.

For instance, I've rarely seen a female usher, but every secretary I've known in the church has been female. Meanwhile greeters and sound operators tend to be both. And, while most security guards might be male, I've seen formidable female ones. A good example is Jeanne Assam, the strategic security guard at the New Life Church in Colorado Springs during the 2007 shooting incident.

18

Understanding Accountability

Let's close with the topic of accountability and *ministerial* accountability in particular. I realize most people have an aversion to this topic for obvious reasons, but I promise that this chapter offers refreshing insights that will really bless you, *wherever* you are at spiritually and *whatever* your calling may be.

Accountability refers to the fact or condition of being accountable. All believers are ultimately accountable to God and will thus stand before Christ at the Judgment Seat to give an account of what we did in the body, whether good or bad (2 Corinthians 5:10-11). Even unbelievers are accountable to their Creator and will hence undergo the Great White Throne Judgment (Revelation 20:11-15).

In the worldwide Church all genuine believers are to be submitted to one another, regardless of sectarian label (Ephesians 5:21). This means that we're accountable to each other — young and old, male and female, spiritually mature and immature, fivefold minister and congregant. Holding each other accountable is relevant to **1.** how we're living and **2.** the accuracy of the doctrines we spread, that is, what we teach/preach from the Scriptures (James 3:1). The effectiveness of this corrective principle is explained in the book of wisdom, "As iron sharpens iron, so one person sharpens another" (Proverbs 27:17).

All Christians — whatever sectarian tag they choose to go by (or not go by) — are to honestly meet at God's Word, which is the blueprint for Christianity regarding all matters of doctrine, practice and morality (2 Timothy 3:16-17 & 1 Corinthians 4:6). We all must be willing to humbly concede to the authority of the God-breathed Scriptures and what they clearly & consistently teach from a New Covenant perspective based on sound hermeneutics. We can all legitimately claim ignorance now and then, but once scriptural revelation is provided we are obligated to make corrections accordingly.

This is true *biblical* accountability. It's simple as ABC.

We could stop here but, as with most topics, there are complexities and therefore...

Some Deeper Questions

What do most Christians automatically think of when they hear the term "accountability"? Likely **1.** being part of a local assembly (& the corresponding sect) and **2.** submitting to the pastoral staff thereof. This is wonderful, but some questions are naturally raised...

What if you legitimately hold a believer from a different camp accountable for teaching false doctrine and prove your case from Scripture, but the person refuses to change his/her belief because their sect supports the erroneous teaching in question? Obviously the leaders of this group will be held accountable by God first and foremost (James 3:1 & Matthew 15:14), but their followers who ignorantly spread the error will also be held responsible to some degree.

What if submitting to a pastor means not fulfilling God's will or God's call? For instance, a subordinate pastor in the Midwest was led to leave the assembly where he was serving and start a ministry in another city far away. The head pastor evidently didn't like this because he arrogantly told him, "If you leave you'll come back crawling on your hands and knees." (Yes, he actually said this). Should the associate pastor **1.** obey this pompous minister who was technically over him or **2.** obey the leading of the Spirit? Thankfully, he did the latter and went on to great fruitbearing service in the Lord.

What if the fivefold minister sins or teaches false doctrine and you can prove it? Is the subordinate believer allowed to correct the one in authority, the one "over" him/her? Both questions are also relevant to when one minister is compelled to correct another minister. Moreover, what if a subordinate minister works for the minister who needs correction? In other words, his/her paycheck depends on good relations with that minister? Wouldn't this hinder positive accountability? Wouldn't this potentially compel the subordinate minister to be a weak "yes man" or "yes woman"?

If it turns out an allegation is true, what do you do if the minister stubbornly refuses to acknowledge it and make corrections after a reasonable period of reflection? What if s/he starts to unjustly persecute you? What if the overseer of the minister in question (assuming there is one) takes a hands-off approach, like Eli did with his two wicked sons who were "in the ministry" (1 Samuel 2:12-17, 27-36)? Do you leave the assembly? Do you leave the sect?

Speaking of overseers: Who oversees the pastor and other fivefold ministers? Who oversees the overseer? Who oversees the one who oversees the overseer; in other words, the one at the top of the spiritual pecking order? (Every sect, ministry or assembly has *someone* at the top). If the answer is God then this shows that official *human* oversight ends — as far as one person being *over* another — when an individual reaches the top of the hierarchy in question. A good example from the Bible is the king of a nation:

> **Do not be in a hurry to leave the king's presence. Do not stand up for a bad cause, for <u>he will do whatever he pleases</u>. [4]Since <u>a king's word is supreme</u>, who can say to him, "What are you doing?"**
>
> **Ecclesiastes 8:3-4**

Of course this wouldn't discount the accountability detailed above: **All believers are accountable to each other based on the truths of the rightly-divided Word of God.** Even kings in Israel — who were in a supreme position — were accountable to the Word of God spoken through a prophet (e.g. 2 Samuel 12:1-14). Unfortunately, but to be expected, ministers stained by arrogance don't like to be corrected by those they consider below them (and no doubt those above them as well, just more so with the former) no matter how humbly and respectfully the correction is offered.

What if you're a fivefold minister — a genuine pastor, teacher, apostle, prophet or evangelist (Ephesians 4:11-13) — and you're led of the Spirit to start your own ministry? I'm talking about believers who have spent *years* — and, more likely, *decades* — learning/training in assemblies & seminaries and the LORD is calling them into a new position in the spirit after much proven service. In such cases, they would be the head of their ministry, much like a business owner is the head of his/her business. If such a minister operates *within* an official sect — like the Assemblies of God or the Southern Baptists — they would still technically have someone over them, like a regional leader.

However, if the individual in question is an independent minister and therefore not part of a sect there would be no official human oversight; in other words, no human would be *above* them in their ministry. But, again, *biblical* accountability would be applicable — **1.** accountability to God and **2.** to fellow believers based on the blueprint of Holy Scripture, which would include accountability to the minister's board/inner circle. Nor would being an independent minister discount mentors in his/her life; such mentors simply wouldn't be "official" overseers appointed by leaders of a particular sect.

Some people reading this might be somewhat sectarian-minded and understandably have difficulty fathoming ministers functioning outside of an official group of Christianity, but Christ himself was an independent minister and people operating independently can be observed even while Yeshua was ministering on Earth (Luke 9:49-50). See chapter **10** for details on the contrast between official ministers and independent ministers.

We talked about subordinate believers (including ministers) becoming "yes men" or "yes women" for the sake of not offending the head minister and thus safeguarding their position. Yet this can happen to the chief minister as well. For instance, when congregants are generous givers it's tempting for pastors to take a passive approach to correction for reasons of self-interest. In other words, they don't confront & correct a certain transgressor because s/he helps pay the rent and they don't want to risk offending them. This isn't right, obviously, but it happens.

Examples of Believers Holding Fellow Believers Accountable

Let's consider a couple of examples of biblical accountability applicable to real life: Say you notice a fellow Christian who's married flirting with a comely woman at work or wherever. This brother may not even go to your assembly, but you can hold him accountable to God's Word by warning him about adultery and the importance of not doing anything that *appears* evil to others (1 Thessalonians 5:22).

Or, say someone is sharing false doctrine in your community, even on Facebook or Twitter; you can hold him/her accountable to the sound doctrine of the rightly-divided word of God. This will likely lead to a Scripture-based dialogue on the topic wherein correction takes place, even if it turns out to be *you* who is corrected. Speaking of which, it's healthy to keep a humble spirit and be open to the possibility that *you* might be wrong if the person you attempt to correct turns out to have fuller knowledge on the topic.

I should add that — since few Christians agree on every jot and tittle (often simply due to sectarian differences) — it's important to major in majors and not in minors. When it comes to God's Word "The main things are the plain things." It's just not profitable to quibble over **disputable matters** (Romans 14:1), not to mention the Bible repeatedly denounces the folly of a **quarrelsome spirit** (Proverbs 17:14, Proverbs 20:3, 2 Timothy 2:14 & Titus 3:9-11).

Both of the above illustrations of accountability are decidedly biblical, as shown in Matthew 18:15-17, Luke 17:3, Galatians 6:1, James 5:19-20 and Proverbs 9:8-9. Please look up these passages and notice that we are instructed to **go to the person** and **confront him/her** in a wise, Spirit-led manner, *not* go to others and gossip about the person and their supposed offense, smearing the individual and poisoning people's minds in the process.

Gossiping about fellow Christians who have (supposedly) offended you poisons believers' minds and thus separates brothers & sisters in the Lord. In short, it causes *division* in the Church. This is a great sin in God's eyes (Proverbs 10:18 & 11:9,12). Matthew 18:15-17 shows that the matter should only be taken to others in the church — *godly* believers who aren't prone to gossip — *if* it turns out the offender is actually guilty of a sin and s/he is stubbornly impenitent.

Here's an example of accountability from my own life regarding possible doctrinal error: A minister friend from another state wrote me and told me he disagreed with a point made in the footnotes of one of my books. I considered his erudite evidence and saw that he was correct and so immediately implemented changes in the corresponding articles. Unfortunately I couldn't change what was printed in the book, but I corrected everything else.

On another occasion, a minister from another continent wrote me to correct what he considered erroneous doctrine in one of our articles. I took the time to hear what he had to say, considered his respectable evidence, and we went back-and-forth a bit. Finally, he modified his viewpoint based on the scriptural data, saying he agreed.

These are actual examples of accountability — brothers & sisters in the Lord prayerfully and carefully holding one another accountable to the blueprint for Christian doctrine, practice and morality, the Holy Scriptures.

More recently a minister from the Philippines wrote me railing about how I was going to "suffer God's wrath," etc. but he was curiously vague concerning his specific accusations. I wrote him back a couple times trying to compel him to state what his issue was and back-up his position with scriptural evidence. He eventually narrowed it down to a particular topic but, even then, 95% of what he said was hollow bluster. He had a spirit of condemnation, covered in chapter **13**. I naturally ignored the irrelevant hot air and focused on the actual subject, offering plenty of Scripture to back-up my position.

It's been about a month and he hasn't written back yet. Why? Because people like this aren't really interested in "examining the Scriptures every day" to find the truth, like the noble Bereans (Acts 17:11). They're only interested in *their* religious tradition and dishing out blustering condo. Speaking of which, let's look at…

Accountability Gone Bad

Biblical accountability is a good thing, but Pharisaical religionists tend to morph it into a negative thing where they constantly concoct dubious accusations based on rash judgments and then poison people's minds against the ones they're supposedly holding accountable; that is, the ones they're accusing. They did this with the sinless Messiah (Matthew 11:19), how much more will they do it with flawed people who genuinely follow the Lord?

The problem with constant questionable accusations is that **it's a trait of the Enemy**. I'm talking about Satan — the "adversary" or "enemy" — who is also called the devil, which is translated from the Greek *diabolos (dee-AB-ol-os)*, meaning **"slanderer."** The term comes from the verb *diaballó (dee-ab-AL-loh)*, meaning "to slander, accuse, defame, complain." On top of this, the Bible plainly describes Satan as "the accuser of our brothers and sisters, who accuses them before our God day and night" (Revelation

12:10). Moreover, Christ called the devil a "**murderer** from the beginning" and "the father of **lies**" (John 8:44).

Do you know a (supposed) brother or sister in the Lord — including "ministers" — who continuously accuse believers (usually behind their backs)? They're behaving like Satan, which isn't a good thing. They're wickedly using their tongue to *murder* others (Proverbs 25:18 & 12:18). Either they're a child of the devil and therefore a counterfeit believer (Matthew 7:15-23 & John 8:42-47) or they're grossly ignorant and misled of the Enemy (2 Timothy 2:24-26).

These are the bad fruits of the devil and the satanic nature, which is the flesh: accusing, slandering, defaming, complaining, lying and murdering. Needless to say, if you know people, groups or organizations that regularly operate in such tactics it tells you everything you need to know — they're "of the devil" — regardless of what respectable position they might hold in the Church.

A good example from the Scriptures is the false apostles who infiltrated the Corinth church and smeared Paul in an attempt to turn the believers against the human founder of the assembly. Being a humble, godly man, Paul was uncomfortable defending himself against their false accusations, but — led of the Spirit — he had no other choice and so became a "fool" by "boasting" of his credentials and defending his ministry (2 Corinthians 11). Observe what Paul concluded about these slandering, accusatory "apostles":

> **For such people are <u>false apostles</u>, deceitful workers, <u>masquerading as apostles of Christ</u>. [14]And no wonder, for <u>Satan himself masquerades as an angel of light</u>.**
>
> **2 Corinthians 11:13-14**

When you come across arrogant individuals who regularly accuse/discredit/slander meek, sincere believers it's a big red flag. As with this case in Corinth, they're false Christians masquerading in key positions in the Church. Don't buy their lies and don't allow your mind to be poisoned against innocent brothers & sisters in the Lord. As Christ said, "By their fruit you will recognize them."

Sectarian "Accountability" that Actually Hinders the Truth

Another kind of accountability gone bad is sectarian "accountability" that, in reality, can hamper the acquisition of truth and its spread. Let me explain…

Christianity consists of hundreds or thousands of sects/camps/denominations, big and small. Each group has some kind of school of training and a means for ministry ordination & licensing. There's nothing wrong with being part of such a camp as long as the group in question remains open to biblical correction and endeavors to fulfill the Great Commission, the problem only enters the picture when believers become sectarian-minded, which is faction-ism, a work of the flesh, as observed in Galatians 5:19-21.[14]

Each of these camps has a "statement of faith," a list of doctrines they consider essential in order to be a member. In other words, the

---

[14] As noted in chapter **7**, the word 'factions' in that passage is *hairesis (HAH-ee-res-is)* in the Greek, meaning "a religious or philosophical sect" and the resulting division it causes. As such, some translations render the word as "divisions," like the English Standard Version. It's a "self-chose opinion" rooted in sectarian loyalty — i.e. one's favored sect — rather than a viewpoint rooted in the rightly-divided Word of God. See the article *Sectarianism — What is It? What's Wrong with It?* at the FOL site for details.

people of every sect agree to agree that certain doctrines are true to the Holy Scriptures and relevant to being a sound Christian. Some of the groups take a harder approach to their list of official doctrines than others, but they all insist that their ministers — their *leaders* — embrace their core doctrines, whatever those might be.

This is healthy as long as the teaching in question is actually biblical, that is, true; however, it becomes unhealthy when it's not. In the latter case, members of the sect **agree to believe a doctrine that is false** and then the leaders hold their members *accountable to* the lie, especially those who are ministers or aspire to be ministers. So if you're a member and discover from the Scriptures that an official doctrine of your sect is false, you'll be expelled from the group or, at least, expelled from ministering in it in a leadership capacity.

Here's a personal example: In 2001 I was getting training and seeking credentials with a certain sect. Carol & I went out to lunch with the head elder when the topic of spiritual gifts came up and he said to me, "If you talk on speaking in tongues it'll be your last sermon." You see? If a sect adheres to false doctrine — in this case the doctrine of cessationism — the hierarchy will hold you accountable to supporting their official doctrines, **even if they are incorrect**. For those not in the know, cessationism is the belief that glossolalia and gifts of the Spirit were done away with once the biblical canon was completed. See the **<u>Appendix</u>** for details.

While you can certainly hold to cessationism and be a respectable Christian loved of the LORD, it will limit your spiritual walk and service since it discourages believers from receiving the baptism of the Holy Spirit & the benefits thereof.[15] The Bible teaches us to

---

[15] For details see the article *Baptism of the Holy Spirit and It's Benefits* at the FOL site.

"eagerly desire" gifts of the Spirit, as observed in 1 Corinthians 12:1,31 and 14:1,39, which would include the gift of glossolalia, aka personal "tongues." Cessationism inspires Christians to do the *exact opposite* of what the Bible plainly instructs us to do — it encourages us to *eagerly deny* spiritual gifts when Holy Scripture encourages us to *eagerly desire* them.

This is accountability gone wrong. It hinders the apprehension & spread of Scriptural truth and perpetuates false doctrine.

I should add that if you are a minister and you get a gig to preach at an assembly of a sect separate from your own you should, generally speaking, respect their official doctrines and wisely operate within the parameters thereof. After all, your goal is to minister to the people — feed them, build them up, heal — not cause undue strife. Of course, if you are **led of the Spirit** to say something that offers doctrinal correction then, by all means, do so (they'll probably never welcome you back though, lol).

Ministers being "Examples" to the Flock

This section ties-in to the topic of accountability so be patient and you'll see why I include it.

A formidable minister I respect preferred small-group assemblies and so criticized pastors of huge fellowships on the grounds that it's impossible to be an example to people you can't spend quality time with because the assembly is so big. It's true that fivefold ministers and elders are called to be *examples* to younger believers, spiritually speaking (1 Peter 5:3, 1 Corinthians 11:1 & 1 Timothy 4:12), but does this mean that spending considerable time with them is the only way to be a good example? If so, how much time does this require? How much privacy is a fivefold minister or elder allowed? Doesn't the Bible say strong believers need to keep some things private to prevent those with weak consciences from stumbling? (Romans 14:22). How far do we take this?

I've functioned in both small group settings and mega-churches and I've seen God work in both. There's nothing wrong with preferring one over the other, but it's wrong to condemn the one you don't favor because **1.** a solid scriptural argument can be made for both and **2.** the LORD is big enough to minister in either setting, and everything in between. Remember, God is not one-dimensional.

Consider Yeshua, who was a daily example to the 12 disciples & friends who traveled with him for three years, and also to the other 72 disciples to a much lesser degree (Luke 10:1,17). Yet how much of an example was he to the *thousands* who came to see him minister? There's *no way* he could regularly spend time with all these people and maintain a tight relationship with the Father and minister effectively; that is, fulfill his calling.

What Christ did was spend quality time with those within his inner circle — particularly Peter, James and John — and they would, in turn, set a similar example with those within their sphere of influence. It's the domino effect of positive social impact. This is precisely how legitimate pastors of big assemblies set the example for their hundreds or thousands of members, not by having bosom buddy relationships with every congregant which, needless to say, is impossible.

Getting back to the minister's criticisms, he chastised pastors of huge churches by alleging they have some sinful practice on the side that they are supposedly hiding. He claimed that this was the real reason they weren't interested in being examples to the flock.

Wow, what a claim and what a blanket statement. Surely no pastor of a small fellowship would ever do this! (sarcasm).

If this were true, then consider the pastor of an assembly I used to go to that had less than 20 attendees: He fell from the ministry after being caught with his hand in the money jar, amongst other dubious activities. Simply put, to **accuse** *all* pastors from huge churches of not setting a proper example and enjoying some sin on the side is uncalled for. This kind of reasoning stems from a legalistic understanding of accountability. Speaking of which…

Eye-Rolling Legalistic "Accountability"

This questionable kind of accountability assumes that believers are all a bunch of weak fools just waiting to rush into sin and hypocrisy, even seasoned fivefold ministers. As such, we need to protect our brothers & sisters by snooping around in their houses and nosing into their personal affairs.

This is the main reason we need "accountability partners," they offer. After all, without the watchful eye of some prying elder we're all doomed to going astray. What a sick mentality. Sure, there will always be immature believers we need to keep an eye on in a protective sense, particularly those in the fundamental stage of spiritual growth, i.e. STAGE TWO, but we have to be careful that this doesn't become a form of bondage or authoritarianism.

It's better to give people the freedom to make a mistake and learn from it than to eye them overbearingly like some mother hen. The former fosters independence while the latter cultivates a dependent, immature spirit. We don't need domineering authoritarians or moronic "accountability partners," we need gatherings of warriors and warrioresses!

As for those "believers" in our midst who can't seem to do anything remotely spiritual without someone hovering over them and twisting their arm, isn't it possible that they're not believers at all? Perhaps they're goats in sheep's clothing, so to speak. *Let 'em go!* The Church is better off without counterfeits. If they're truly genuine they'll come back at some point of their own accord.

This will come as a shock to those with a legalistic understanding of accountability, but there are numerous areas of believers' lives — including fivefold ministers — that are no one's business. For instance, what a person does in the bathroom is a thoroughly private matter. Moreover, what I do when I go out with my wife or what I enjoy for recreation is no one's business but mine, Carol's and the Lord's, unless of course iniquity is involved. It's the same thing with how people choose to make a living, assuming it's not criminal, or what vehicle they decide to drive or what style of clothes they wear, assuming they're not inappropriately immodest.

We'll address faultfinding & nosiness further in a moment, let's first look at…

Submitting to Ministers / Submitting to Each Other

The Bible instructs believers to submit to their spiritual leaders, like pastors & teachers, so that their service will be a joy and not a burden (Hebrews 13:17). Diligent servant-leaders should be honored, especially those who preach & teach (1 Thessalonians 5:12 & 1 Timothy 5:17), but there's a healthy way to submit to them and an unhealthy way.

For instance, it's unhealthy to submit in an absolute sense, as covered in chapter **11**. If your spiritual leader told you to jump off a cliff, should you do it? If he/she encouraged you to engage in sexual immorality, would you do it? If s/he taught blatant false doctrine and demanded you accept it, should you? Obviously not, so there are wise limits to this kind of submission.

Christ is the "Chief Shepherd" in the worldwide Church whereas fivefold ministers are *under*-shepherds (1 Peter 5:1-5). This shows that ministers are **accountable to the Lord** (Luke 12:42-48).

I encourage **submitting to one another in Christ**, as plainly instructed in the New Testament (Ephesians 5:21 & 1 Corinthians 16:15-16). Obviously the most fruitbearing believers would rank at the top of the list, which presumably includes your spiritual leader(s), although not necessarily. I should specify that by "fruitbearing" I'm talking about bearing fruit of the spirit as opposed to works of the flesh (Galatians 5:19-23). The Lord pointed out that you can distinguish a true minister from a false minister by their fruit (Matthew 7:15-23). Do you see a "minister" constantly faultfinding, accusing and slandering other believers? It tells you everything you need to know.

I emphasize this so that submitting to ministers, like pastors, isn't a one-way street, which can lead to abuse. In short, the minister is accountable to subordinate believers as well as those over him/her in the spiritual pecking order. This is *why* Paul stressed this by the Spirit — so that pastors & other fivefold ministers don't become arrogant and unaccountable in their top positions at ministries. Remember, **God *opposes* the proud** (James 4:6 & 1 Peter 5:5). This brings up…

Who Oversees the Minister?

We considered this issue earlier, but let's look at it in more detail here. Who oversees the pastor? Usually someone higher up in the pastor's organization that doesn't regularly attend the assembly in question, like a regional leader. It may also be pastors from other fellowships in the area who may or may not be part of the minister's sect. How closely do these people oversee the pastor? How often do they communicate? Not all that closely or often, right?

Furthermore, who oversees those who oversee the pastor? I'm talking about ministers higher up in the chain of authority of the sect in question. My point is that at some juncture in spiritual growth close human oversight becomes minuscule, even irrelevant. Why? Because the believers have matured. They've established a relationship with God; they walk in the spirit and not in the flesh; and they're quick to humbly 'fess up when they do miss it (1 John 1:8-9 & Matthew/Luke 3:8). This is in line with what a minister friend told me:

> *My job is to become unnecessary in the life of the believer.*

This should be the goal of *all* ministers: disciple people to the point where they walk with God of their own accord, guided by the Holy Spirit, and have no need of close pastoral oversight. If some ministerial work needs done, like praying for a relative in the hospital or sharing the Word with someone, the disciple doesn't call the pastor or some other minister but rather does it himself/herself. Unfortunately, some ministers foster a *dependent* spirit with their congregants because — consciously or subconsciously — they don't want to lose them and, in some cases, they relish having people dependent on them. This is an unhealthy and unscriptural attitude to say the least.

As noted earlier, not all fivefold ministers are "official" in the sense that they belong to an official sect, some are independent. Ministers who are independent are just as necessary as "official" ministers, but both can be corrupted, as detailed in chapter **10**. Independent ministers are usually non-sectarian and don't function within a specific sect and thus they don't operate within a delineated authority structure as official ministers do.

Yet this doesn't negate that independent ministers are accountable since **1.** they are accountable to the LORD & the God-breathed Scriptures first and foremost and **2.** to the body of Christ at large, which includes their inner circle of believers and mentors. Keep in mind that **most effective correction takes place through (1) having a humble, teachable heart that craves greater knowledge and (2) the simple process of learning**. Direct face-to-face correction is secondary.[16]

Consider Paul, who left the structure of the Jerusalem church and went off to minister to the Gentiles, as led of the Spirit (Acts 18:6, 26:15-23, Galatians 2:7 & Romans 15:15-16). His three long missionary journeys comprised almost two decades of his life, which includes the years he was a prisoner wherein he wrote the four prison epistles.

Paul didn't function within an official authority structure during this time. In fact, he was the top Christian authority in these travels as he preached the message of reconciliation, started assemblies across the landscape and wrote epistles by the Spirit, but this didn't

---

[16] For details see the article *Disciple — What is it? (The answer might surprise you)* at the FOL site.

mean he wasn't accountable. Again, he was accountable to the LORD and fellow believers in general (whom were technically "under" him, by the way).

It's also important to point out that Paul didn't view any leader in the Jerusalem church as "God Jr.", as shown here:

> **As for <u>those who seemed to be important—whatever they were makes no difference to me; God does not show favoritism—they added nothing to my message.</u> [7]On the contrary, they recognized that I had been entrusted with the task of preaching the gospel to the uncircumcised, just as Peter had been to the circumcised. [8]For God, who was at work in Peter as an apostle to the circumcised, was also at work in me as an apostle to the Gentiles. [9]James, Peter and John, <u>those reputed to be pillars</u>** [of the Church]**, gave me and Barnabas the right hand of fellowship when they recognized the grace given to me. They agreed that we should go to the Gentiles, and they to the circumcised.**
>
> **Galatians 2:6-9**

Whilst James, Peter and John walked closely with Jesus when he ministered on Earth, Paul clearly didn't view them as spiritual authorities in the absolute sense. The Mighty Christ is the only head of the worldwide Church, i.e. the spiritually-regenerated "called-out ones" across the globe (Ephesians 1:22 & Colossians 1:18). Was Paul belittling these leaders in these verses? No, he was providing balanced perspective **by the Spirit** so no person or persons in the body of Christ come to be considered infallible and untouchable, like a pope; rather "Christ is all and in all" (Colossians 3:11 & Romans 10:12).

As noted in chapter **10**, Jesus Christ was an independent minister. While he was a Hebrew believer who habitually went to synagogue, he didn't **identify with** any of the various Israelite factions of the 1st Century, such as the Pharisees, Sadducees, Herodians, Essenes, Zealots and so on. Nor did he operate strictly within the parameters of such a group. Being independent and dedicated to God's Word above all, the Messiah wasn't biased based on sectarian loyalties. Believers today shouldn't either.

John the Baptist was another independent minister. For those not in the know, the New Testament *started* with John (Luke 16:16). He hailed from the desert wilderness wherein his clothes were made of camel hair and he survived on locusts & wild honey (Matthew 3:1-11). Contrary to the claims of some, John didn't identify with the Essenes (like those at Qumrân) since the differences between John's message/activities, and those of this sect of Judaism, are as significant as any alleged similarities. Yet this doesn't mean John didn't fellowship with them on occasion wherein accountability worked both ways.

The obvious weakness of being an official minister is that you can become a pathetic "yes man" or "yes woman" who's afraid to call out false doctrines/practices/corruptions or correct someone who's over them in the authority chain for fear of losing favor and their position; or even being defrocked altogether.

Martin Luther, for example, dared to speak out against a number of his denomination's unbiblical doctrines & practices and so he lost his job and credentials, was branded a heretic and banished to live in hiding, his books were burned and Pope Adrian VI declared him to be the antichrist.

Why did Luther do something so costly? **Because he was accountable to the LORD and the Word of God first and**

foremost (James 3:1). As he was believed to have said, "Unless I am convinced by Scripture and plain reason — I do not accept the authority of popes and councils for they have contradicted each other — my conscience is captive to the Word of God… Here I stand, I cannot do otherwise." Notice that he did not consider himself accountable to popes or councils, but rather to the authority of the LORD and the God-breathed Scriptures (2 Timothy 3:16-17).

Consider these contrasting examples of official leaders in Israel: After King David's adultery with Bathsheba and his failed attempts to get valiant Uriah to sleep with his wife so as to cover up his sin, David contacted Israel's military commander, Joab, and instructed him to put Uriah in the front line where the fighting was fiercest and then have the other soldiers withdraw so Uriah would die in battle. This is murder in an indirect form, but murder nevertheless.

Joab *should* have rejected this wicked order since Uriah was a noble, brave warrior, but he instead chose to be a pathetic "yes man" (2 Samuel 11:14-21). Shortly later, the prophet Nathan refused to be like this. He boldly confronted David's corruption and spoke the truth, come what may (2 Samuel 12:1-14). Joab failed to hold the King accountable whereas Nathan did.

When you see corruption in the leadership of the body of Christ you can either weakly go along with it, like Joab, or hold the person accountable whatever the cost, like Nathan. If you choose the former you'll have to answer for it at the Judgment Seat because the Lord will hold you **accountable**.

The obvious challenge for independent ministers is their lack of an official hierarchy and their potential for creative interpretations of the Scriptures (as if official sects don't have their share of questionable positions, such as "once saved always saved"[17] and the grossly erroneous amillennialism[18]). However, humble submission to the LORD, the rightly-divided Word of God and the body of Christ at large alleviates this issue wherein needed corrections are regularly made.

Of course, being part of a reputable official sect and functioning under a designated chain of authority isn't a guarantee of proper accountability and righteousness. The pastor I mentioned earlier who was ousted after he got caught with his hand in the proverbial cookie jar was from the Assemblies of God, which is the last thing from a loose sect. Several members of the congregation and inner circle were members of his extended family and yet this pastor went quite a long time before being found out, confronted and disciplined (although it's certainly commendable that this eventually happened).

It goes without saying that, if someone *wants* to practice sin as a lifestyle, they'll find a way to do it and hide it, whether they operate within an official sect/assembly and the power structure thereof or not.

Also, as noted earlier, just because an official sect supports a doctrine, this doesn't make the teaching true. Furthermore, if it *is* a false doctrine it doesn't make it okay for ministers in that sect to spread the erroneous teaching, even though it's advocated by their sect. While their fellow ministers may applaud them, they will be

---

[17] While the Bible certainly supports eternal security (John 10:27-30), it clearly does not support *unconditional* eternal security (2 Timothy 2:12, Hebrews 10:26-27, 2 Peter 2:20-21 & Galatians 5:19-21). For details see *Once Saved Always Saved?* (and its follow-up article) at the FOL site.

[18] If you're not familiar with amillennialism see the corresponding article at the FOL site.

held accountable for false doctrine when they stand before the Lord (James 3:1).

Legalists are Unreasonably Judgmental FAULTFINDERS

Holding one another accountable is beneficial, but I think it's necessary to include a warning about faultfinding.

Those who tend to excessively harp on accountability (always in the clichéd, simplistic sense) also tend to be hell-bent on picking out people's flaws and condemning them accordingly. They're **faultfinders**, *im*pure and simple, which is a fleshly characteristic according to the Scriptures (Jude 1:16 & Romans 15:7). Even worse, they're often guilty of the very things they criticize in others. This isn't *righteous* judging, like Paul's judgment and low-key public rebuke of Peter's legalism in Galatians 2:11-14, but rather *hypocritical* judging. Notice what Jesus said about this type of judging:

> **Do not judge, or you too will be judged. [2] For in the same way you judge others, you will be judged, and with the measure you use, it will be measured to you. [3] Why do you look at the speck of sawdust in your brother's eye and pay no attention to the plank in your own eye? [4] How can you say to your brother, 'Let me take the speck out of your eye,' when all the time there is a plank in your own eye? [5] <u>You hypocrite</u>, first take the plank out of your own eye, and <u>then</u> you will see clearly to remove the speck from your brother's eye."**
>
> **Matthew 7:1-5**

Christ wasn't denouncing *righteous* judging, like judging a fellow believer's bad fruit and offering a corrective word, as when Paul reprimanded Peter which, by the way, is a good example of biblical accountability. The Lord was condemning *hypocritical* judging — criticizing others for things that the criticizer himself or herself practices.

It goes without saying that being a grumpy **faultfinder** is a big red flag. Those preoccupied with faultfinding are either immature believers stuck in STAGE TWO or they're counterfeit believers actually lost in STAGE ONE.

Closing Thoughts on Accountability

"Iron sharpens iron" (Proverbs 27:17) and "many advisers bring success" (Proverbs 15:22) with the greatest advisor being the Holy Spirit (John 14:26-28, 16:13 & 1 John 2:27). Believers are to submit to the LORD & each other and therefore are accountable to one another based on the truths of the Word of God (Ephesians 5:21).

But, to be balanced, here's an important axiom to consider: All people are flawed and have a downside, even the best of us — even the greatest minister or hero you can name (Psalm 130:3-4, Ecclesiastes 7:20, Proverbs 20:9 & 1 John 1:8). A big time minister said he has hanged out with the top international ministers you can cite and he said, without exception, they were all flawed and had a downside, one way or another.

As such, it makes best sense to have as few people *over* you as possible in your endeavors, particularly as you mature. This is the Conservative perspective wherein government should be small and limited whereas the **LIE**beral perspective is that government should be huge with endless (useless) bureaucrats.

(By "**LIE**beral" I'm not referring to classical liberals, who tend to be kind-hearted, reasonable people. I'm referring to modern, radical Leftwingers who have taken over liberalism in America. Since practically everything these people believe and preach is based on a lie, they can more accurately be called **LIE**berals.[19] A good example is their support of biological men identifying as female and then competing in women's sports wherein they often beat the *real* females. Leftwingers celebrate such absurdities and cajole others to do likewise).

In any ministry or business there's a head with a vision, along with the corresponding inner circle/board. If you can't agree with the head's vision then you should leave, otherwise there will be division. I'm not talking about condoning sin or gross error. If you see either you should obviously confront the individual as led of the Spirit, keeping in mind that there's always a profitable and unprofitable way to do this.

The New Testament encourages believers to humbly submit to the heads of the ministry they're involved with (Hebrews 13:17) and honor diligent servant-leaders (1 Thessalonians 5:12-13) "so that their work will be a joy, not a burden." If you *can't* do this, or can no longer do this, please leave and go somewhere that you can agree with the vision or — if led of the Spirit — start your own work, like Paul, who was led to conduct his own ministry to the Gentiles. In the latter event you'll be the head of your ministry, but you'll still be accountable to **1.** the LORD & the God-breathed

---

[19] Keep in mind that Christ Himself called people names on justified occasions, like "hypocrites" (fakes), "snakes," "blind fools," "whitewashed tombs" and so forth (e.g. Matthew 23:13-33). It's a form of tough love.

Scriptures and **2.** the worldwide body of Christ based on biblical truth.

Ultimately, every believer will **give account** of his/her life at the Judgment Seat:

> **For we must all appear before the judgment seat of Christ, so that each of us may receive what is due us for the things done while in the body, whether good or bad.**
> **[11] Since, then, we know what it is to fear the Lord, we try to persuade others. What we are is plain to God, and I hope it is also plain to your conscience.**
>
> **2 Corinthians 5:10-11**

Closing Word

I trust you have a better understanding of those in the body of Christ called to the fivefold ministry. There are five separate gifts and therefore those who serve in ministry are not all pastors that shepherd local believers at the fellowship down the street.

I also trust that you have an improved grasp of the dynamics of ministers, ministries and believers. Some ministers are 'official' while others are independent.

Although each of the five ministry gifts in the Church are of eminent value and instrumental to healthy spiritual growth, there's potential for folly and corruption, of which you are now better aware and prepared to handle if abuse rears its ugly head.

Everything we've talked about is applicable to standard assemblies and more atypical ones, conventional ministries and unconventional ones. In other words, the principles and scenarios are just as much relevant to a handful of believers in a house or at the mall (Matthew 18:20) as the formidable 'official' church on the corner.

To illustrate, I was once hiking the local Nelson Ledges with a friend wherein we coincidentally came across a minister I know who happened to be counseling a young man in a remote section of the park. These two were having a church meeting in the forest and the minister was fulfilling his service for God's Kingdom. This shows that effective ministry can occur anywhere, anytime and not just in the hallowed halls of a church building.

One reason this is important to grasp is because *some* people simply refuse to go to a conventional church structure for anything. So you'll have to reach them where they're at or where they're comfortable.

May the LORD bless you in your service as you continually draw closer to God, seek the truth, and apply what you've learned.

Amen.

<u>Appendix</u>

What is Cessationism and is it Biblical?

Cessationism *(seh-SAY-shun-izm)* is the belief that gifts of the Spirit (1 Corinthians 12:4-11) ceased by the end of the 1st Century when the last of the original apostles passed away and the biblical canon was completed. While most adherents of cessationism believe God still performs miracles, they don't believe that the LORD works miracles through the gifts of the Spirit any longer.

Nor do they believe that the ministerial offices of the apostle and prophet — with the signs & wonders thereof — are in operation today; they believe these ceased when what they call the 'Apostolic Age' ended with the 1st Century. Cessationists suggest that 1 Corinthians 13:8-12 supports this theory. Let's read the passage from two different translations:

> **Love never fails. But where there are <u>prophecies, they will cease</u>; where there are <u>tongues, they will be stilled</u>; where there is knowledge, it will pass away. [9] For we know in part and we**

prophesy in part, [10] but <u>when completeness comes, what is in part disappears.</u> [11] When I was a child, I talked like a child, I thought like a child, I reasoned like a child. When I became a man, I put the ways of childhood behind me. [12]<u>For now we see only a reflection as in a mirror; then we shall see face to face. Now I know in part; then I shall know fully,</u> even as I am fully known.

1 Corinthians 13:8-12 (NIV)

Love never ends. As for <u>prophecies, they will pass away;</u> as for <u>tongues, they will cease;</u> as for knowledge, it will pass away. [9] For we know in part and we prophesy in part, [10] but <u>when the perfect comes, the partial will pass away.</u> [11]When I was a child, I spoke like a child, I thought like a child, I reasoned like a child. When I became a man, I gave up childish ways. [12] <u>For now we see in a mirror dimly, but then face to face. Now I know in part;</u> then I shall know fully, even as I have been fully known.

1 Corinthians 13:8-12 (ESV)

Cessationists argue that this passage contrasts life before and after the biblical canon was completed, but that's not what it's talking about and obviously so. The text contrasts our life on this Earth where "we see in a mirror dimly" with life on the other side of glory being "face to face" with our Creator: *now* we only "know in part" whereas *then* we shall "know fully" even as we are "fully known" now by the LORD (verse 12).

The "mirror" Paul references is translated from the Greek word *esoptron (ES-op-tron)*, which is not like the mirrors we have today;

it was a looking-glass made of highly polished metal that produced an indistinct image of the person viewing it. Paul relates this to our time on Earth during this "present evil age" (Galatians 1:4): Compared to life on the other side of glory where we'll see our Creator face-to-face, life on this Earth is like seeing a poor reflection in an inferior mirror of the 1st Century. In eternity we shall "know fully" instead of "knowing in part" as we do now; spiritual gifts, like prophecy and glossolalia, will no longer be needed in the perfect eternal age to come. I'm talking about the eternal age of the New Heavens and New Earth, the home of righteousness (2 Peter 3:13 & Revelation 21-22).

Since fivefold ministers in the 1st Century were known to flow in the gifts of the Spirit (1 Corinthians 12:4-11) — particularly apostles, prophets and evangelists (2 Corinthians 12:12 & Acts 8:4-7, 8:26-40, 21:8) — cessationists suggest that the offices of apostles and prophets have ceased in the Church since the 1st Century, but they're okay with evangelists as long as they're revivalists or missionaries who lack any evidence of the gifts of the Spirit.

The obvious problem with this belief is that **nowhere in the New Testament do we see any indication that these offices would cease to exist by the end of the 1st Century**. The evidence cessationists desperately *try* to amass is so weak I'm not even going to cite any. It smacks of grasping for straws.

Furthermore, cessationists seem to emphasize how true apostles walked with the Lord on Earth, i.e. Christ's former 12 disciples, like James, Peter and John (minus Judas Iscariot, of course). But Paul is the preeminent apostle of the New Testament who wrote far more epistles than any other apostle and he *didn't* walk with the Lord when Christ ministered on Earth. If the Lord can call Paul to be an apostle well after his ascension, he can certainly call other believers to such positions — to this day.

The biggest problem with the religious doctrine of cessationism is that it encourages believers to *deny* what the New Testament Scriptures plainly instruct us to eagerly desire: Believers are exhorted to "**eagerly desire**" spiritual gifts (1 Corinthians 12:1,31 & 14:1,39) while cessationism encourages believers to do **the precise opposite**.

This of course creates a spirit of **unbelief** when it comes to miracles, like divine healing. The problem with this is that our New Covenant with God is a covenant (contract) of faith and **we receive from the LORD based on our faith**, i.e. *belief* (Hebrews 11:1,6 & Luke 8:43-48). This explains why Christ was hampered from performing miracles in his hometown when he ministered there (Matthew 13:54-58). Do you want to be hampered from receiving miracles in your life? Then, by all means, embrace the doctrine of cessationism because it will kill your faith real quick.

I should add that, while cessationism is a false doctrine, it's not an issue of eternal salvation. If a believer or sect embraces this doctrine it doesn't mean they're *not* fellow believers, loved by the Lord. It just means their faith — their level of belief based on the false doctrine of cessationism — won't allow them to "eat everything" the gospel of Christ has to offer; in this case, spiritual gifts and the blessings thereof. (Romans 14:1-6).

Those of us with fuller understanding are *not* to look down on those with the lesser because it would be arrogant. Similarly, the one with the lesser revelation must not condemn the one with the fuller. On the contrary, we are to "accept one another… just as Christ accepted [us], in order to bring praise to God" (Romans

15:7). You could insert any non-essential doctrine or issue into this scenario and it would apply.

What perpetuates the false doctrine of cessationism? Certainly not what the New Testament teaches! Rigid sectarianism is the main cause. Believers grow-up spiritually in assemblies/sects that deny the gifts of the Spirit, as well as the offices of apostle & prophet, and the congregants who are eventually called into vocational ministry — pastors, teachers and evangelists (minus gifts of the Spirit) — will then teach/preach the same error to the believers entrusted to their care. It becomes 'tradition' in their sect as the decades or centuries pass.

Another factor is that people tend to prefer the mundane to the supernatural. The mundane is more reliable to them because it's more comfortable in regards to where they're at spiritually and less challenging to their faith. In other words, it's *easier* to be a cessationist.

For instance, it's easier for a minister to just teach/preach a sermon, counsel congregants and pray for believers before they have surgery than mess around with gifts of the Spirit or teach believers to simply pray for healing & actually believe it. I'm not condemning anyone here; I'm just sharing the way it is.

Furthermore, the deeper a minister or any believer goes in God the more reliant on the Holy Spirit & the supernatural they'll be, like when it comes to needing a healing. This naturally results in persecution from believers who are less spiritually mature or who, for whatever reason, don't "eat everything." They'll mock you as a "holy roller" and the like because the deeper things of God freak them out.

So there's pressure in the Church, generally speaking, to keep one's Christianity as mundane as possible. And this is why cessationism is so appealing in the body of Christ.

Lastly, continuationism is the name theologians have given for the scriptural belief that gifts of the Spirit have been available to the Church since it began and the offices of charismatic fivefold ministries never ceased, e.g. apostle and prophet. Those who embrace continuationism are "continuationists" (actually they're simply believers who happen to *believe* what the Bible plainly teaches).

The only thing that hinders gifts of the Spirit and charismatic fivefold offices in the body of Christ today is **unbelief**. And the false doctrine of cessationism feeds this unbelief.

<u>Bibliography</u>

Brown, Francis/Driver, S.R./Briggs, Charles A. *Brown-Driver-Briggs Lexicon.* Peabody: Hendrickson Publishers, 1994

Bullinger, Ethelbert W. A Critical Lexicon and Concordance to the English and Greek New Testament. Grand Rapids: Zondervan Publishing House, 1975

Deligiannides, Hariton. *Pastor's Handbook: Weddings and Funerals.* Retrieved from https://nocompromiseradio.com/2017/08/pastors-handbook-weddings-funerals/. 2017

Helps Word-Studies Lexicon. Retrieved from Biblehub.com. 1987, 2011

Kirkwood, David. *Your Best Year Yet!* Pittsburgh: Ethnos Press, 1996

LORD, The. *The Amplified Bible.* Grand Rapids: Zondervan, 1987

LORD, The. *English Standard Version (ESV). Holy Bible.* Chicago: Crossway, 2001

LORD, The. *The International Standard Version New Testament.* Highlands Ranch: Davidson Press, 1998

LORD, The. *King James Version. Holy Bible.* Iowa Falls: World Bible Publishers

LORD, The. *New International Version (Revised). Holy Bible.* Nashville: Holman, 2011

LORD, The. *New King James Version Study Bible: Second Edition.* Nashville: Thomas Nelson, 2012

LORD, The. *Quest Study Bible: New International Version.* Grand Rapids: Zondervan, 2003

Strong, James. *Strong's Exhaustive Concordance.* Grand Rapids: Baker, 1991

Vine, W.E. *Vine's Expository Dictionary of Biblical Words.* Cambridge: Nelson, 1985

Waren, Dirk. *Legalism Unmasked*. Youngstown: Soaring Eagle Press, 2013/2018

Fountain of Life
Teaching Ministry
(Psalm 36:9)

The mission of Fountain of Life is to **set the captives FREE** by **reaching the world** with the **life-changing truths of God's Word**, the **power of the Holy Spirit** and the **Awesome News of the message of Jesus Christ**.

**We're calling Spiritual Warriors all over the Earth
to partner with us on this mission!**

Books by Dirk Waren:

The Believer's Guide to FORGIVENESS & WARFARE
Legalism Unmasked
HELL KNOW! (full and condensed versions)
SHEOL KNOW! (full and condensed versions)
The Four Stages of Spiritual Growth
ANGELS: Their Purpose and Your Responsibility
THE LAW and the Believer
The SIX BASIC DOCTRINES of Christianity
GRACE: What is It? How Do You Grow in It?
How to Handle OFFENSES: Personal & Criminal
WOMEN in Ministry ...in God's Service
The FIVEFOLD MINISTRY Gifts: Apostle, Prophet, Evangelist, Pastor, Teacher
Solomon's SONG OF SONGS: Questions & Answers

9 798218 026738